"You don't need to be Mennonite to cook this food and eat it. *Mennonite Girls Can Cook* has great photos that accompany each recipe and a lot of comfort food. I'm getting hungry now!"

SOPHIE LUI, MORNING NEWS ANCHOR FOR GLOBAL BC

"Whether you are of Mennonite background or not, you will don your apron and head into the kitchen to make these simple, delectable country recipes spiced with memories and inspirational thoughts."

ROSE MURRAY, AUTHOR OF TEN COOKBOOKS, INCLUDING *A TASTE OF CANADA*

"Commitment to faith, family, friends, and fellowship is the very soul of this book. However, it is the food that binds all these ingredients together to create an endearing sense of coming home."

LAURIE GOETZ, MANAGER OF TEN THOUSAND VILLAGES, WINNIPEG, MANITOBA

"This is the best cookbook I have seen in my life, showing not only family recipes and gorgeous photos but the life and heritage of the authors. These authors also capture the essence of stewardship, sharing their passion, wisdom, and philosophies, and at the same time ensuring environmentally conscious agriculture."

PETER G. ANDRES, OWNER OF POPLAR GROVE ARBOUR AND PRESIDENT OF BRITISH COLUMBIA HAZELNUT GROWERS ASSOCIATION

"This new book is sure to inspire many others to explore the wonderful world of *Paska*, *Vereniki*, *Borscht*, and *Portzelky*. With the publication of this book, the secret is out— Mennonite girls really can cook!"

ED FAST, MEMBER OF PARLIAMENT, ABBOTSFORD, BRITISH COLUMBIA

"Between each line of this delightful book is written the desire to feed hungry children. Lovella and this amazing group of authors share their courage, passion, and tenacity. We count it a privilege to be part of fulfilling their dream by selling their book and donating 100 percent of our profits to fill the empty bowls of little ones in Romania."

WENDY AND DAVE MURRAY, OWNERS OF WINKS HOME GARDEN & GIFTS, CHILLIWACK, BRITISH COLUMBIA

"*Mennonite Girls Can Cook* is like opening up your grandma's personal cookbook. It is overflowing with comfort food."

SHARON WILLIAMS, BLOGGER, *SIMPLY REBEKAH*, DANVILLE, KENTUCKY

"What a mouth-watering journey through my childhood, paging through this splendid collection of Mennonite recipes and photographs! I've eaten from a lot of other menus since then, but this food still *schmecks* (tastes) like no other food *schmecks*!"

ANDREAS SCHROEDER, AUTHOR OF *RENOVATING HEAVEN* AND *THE MENNONITES: A PICTORIAL HISTORY OF THEIR LIVES IN CANADA*

"At a time when there is renewed interest in cooking and wonderful fresh food, *Mennonite Girls Can Cook* offers excellent, time-proven recipes. But it also celebrates our Mennonite heritage of faith, food, family, friends, and fellowship."

HELEN ROSE PAULS, MENNONITE HISTORICAL SOCIETY OF BRITISH COLUMBIA AND MENNONITE BRETHREN HERALD

"Photographed amazingly, the warmth of the girls' hospitality comes right off of the pages. When I need a recipe, I go to *Mennonite Girls Can Cook* because I know it can be trusted for taste and presentation."

AUDREY NEUFELD, NEUFELD FARMS, ABBOTSFORD, BRITISH COLUMBIA

"*Mennonite Girls Can Cook* takes the mystery out of 'enough flour to make a soft dough' from Oma's time-honored recipes. The authors' passionate love of beautifully presented, wholesome food leaps off every page and is sure to inspire the next generation."

CHARLOTTE LEPP, LEPP FARM MARKET, ABBOTSFORD, BRITISH COLUMBIA

"This delightful book is more than just recipes. It's about the authors' faith, families, and life experiences. Mennonite cooking is a wholesome, healthy, and economical way to feed your family, or to share the joy of hospitality with friends."

LUCY LEID, AUTHOR OF *COUNTRYSIDE COOKING AND CHATTING*

"*Mennonite Girls Can Cook* sends you on an imaginary journey back into the lives of our ancestors. As the authors share their personal stories behind the recipes, you want to become part of this large Mennonite family of special cooks."

ESTHER SHANK, AUTHOR OF *MENNONITE COUNTRY-STYLE RECIPES AND KITCHEN SECRETS*

"This cookbook is the culmination of a great virtual potluck that began when ten women started blogging their favorite recipes. These old favorites are now gathered along with new recipes in an easy-to-use book."

MARSHALL KING, COLUMNIST FOR *THE ELKHART TRUTH*

Traditions of Food and Faith

MENNONITE
GIRLS
CAN COOK

Lovella Schellenberg   Anneliese Friesen

Judy Wiebe   Betty Reimer

Bev Klassen   Charlotte Penner

Ellen Bayles   Julie Klassen

Kathy McLellan   Marg Bartel

HERALD
PRESS

Harrisonburg, Virginia

Herald Press
PO Box 866, Harrisonburg, Virginia 22803
www.HeraldPress.com

Library and Archives Canada Cataloguing in Publication
　　Mennonite girls can cook / Lovella Schellenberg ... [et al.].
Includes index.
ISBN 978-0-8361-9553-8
　　1. Mennonite cooking. 2. Cookbooks. I. Schellenberg, Lovella, 1959-
TX715.6.M46 2011　641.5'66　C2011-900519-0

Mennonite Girls Can Cook
© 2011 by Herald Press, Harrisonburg, Virginia 22803. 800-245-7894.
　　All rights reserved.
Library of Congress Control Number: 2011920439
Canadiana Entry Number: C2011-900519-0
International Standard Book Number: 978-0-8361-9553-8
Printed in Canada
Design by Reuben Graham

24 23 22 21 20　　　　　　　14 13 12 11 10 9 8

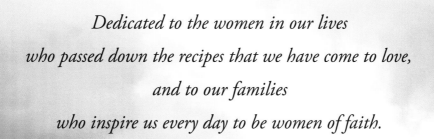

Dedicated to the women in our lives
who passed down the recipes that we have come to love,
and to our families
who inspire us every day to be women of faith.

All author royalties from *Mennonite Girls Can Cook*
will be donated to charity to feed hungry children.

Contents

Foreword

I feel honored to have been asked to write the foreword for this wonderful cookbook. These Mennonite girls truly love their heritage, as I do my own Amish heritage. Our ancestors left us many treasures. Among them are recipes that come from our mothers, grandmothers, and great-grandmothers.

Just as these ten Mennonite girls are doing, I enjoy passing my own Amish heritage down to my children. I hope someday they will do the same. Our heritage is a very important part of our lives, and along with it comes the foods we remember and grew fond of as children. These favorite foods tend to find a way into our hearts.

In *Mennonite Girls Can Cook* I see similarities to my own favorite family recipes. The refrigerator potato rolls, except for the eggs, are very much like the sourdough bread that I make. The noodles in this book, too, are like my own. Then there are the recipes that I had never heard of but am now eager to try, like *Obst Moos*.

Some of the more unusual recipes in this collection reflect the authors' Russian Mennonite roots, whereas my recipes show my own Swiss-German Amish heritage. Yet these authors and I share a similar Anabaptist faith heritage.

As I read each girl's story I notice several things we have in common in our traditions. Each of us was taught that the most important part of our heritage is the wonderful conviction that God should always come first in our lives.

The hospitality that the girls write about was also taught to me. I still remember how, when I was a little girl, a homeless man would sometimes stop by our house. Mother was always willing to feed him. This man would walk from one Amish home to another to eat and sleep. My parents always taught us never to refuse anyone if they were hungry and asked for food to eat.

My mother would always ask friends or family who dropped in around mealtime to stay and eat with us. The authors of this cookbook share many similar stories of friends and family dropping in around mealtime and being invited to stay and share in the bounty.

From reading *Mennonite Girls Can Cook* I can tell that each of the authors has a welcoming home and a welcoming heart. I hope that this book will be a great success and that the royalties the girls have donated will help many needy children. I wish each one—Lovella, Anneliese, Judy, Betty, Bev, Charlotte, Ellen, Julie, Kathy, and Marg—God's blessings.

>   —***Lovina Eicher***
>   Author of the syndicated column *The Amish Cook* and cookbooks *The Amish Cook at Home*, *The Amish Cook's Anniversary Book*, and *The Amish Cook's Baking Book*

Preface

Family, Food, and Friendship

As a youngster, I was convinced my mom made the best chicken noodle soup ever, and I loved spreading icing on her thick slices of *Paska*. My sister-in-law Mary made the most impressive stacks of transparent apple pies for her freezer every summer. I looked forward to babysitting on Saturday mornings because Dolly, another sister-in-law, would leave me with recipes, ingredients, and free reign in her kitchen. A third sister-in-law, Heidi, taught me pure hospitality by regularly inviting people home to join their family after church.

We are surrounded by fond recollections of times shared with families and friends around the table. Pause for a moment and savor your own food memories: whose potato salad did you most anticipate? In whose home could you always find a fresh pot of coffee?

Supper invitations from our friends and family are delightfully anticipated. Food and friendship go hand in hand, and are appreciated, whether the call is to come roast wieners over an open fire or to share special meals that have been prepared with care.

The girls and I are just ten of many cooks who enjoy serving meals to our friends and families using the recipes that have been handed down and shared with us along the way. Sharing recipes and menu ideas are wonderful ways to forge new friendships.

The Mennonite Girls Connection

When I posted a recipe for *Paska* on my personal blog in time for Easter 2007, I had no idea that some of the readers would eventually become "the girls" of *Mennonite Girls Can Cook*. Judy emailed me first, reminding me that we were second cousins by marriage. Soon we were comparing family recipes, noting how similar they were. Within weeks, Judy and her longtime friend, Marg, reconnected over coffee, only to learn that they had started their own blogs and had both discovered my posted *Paska* recipe.

As a blogger, I saw opportunities within my readership to "whitewash my fence," as Tom Sawyer would say, by inviting my friends to share favorite recipes, which would be featured along with a picture. Charlotte sent me her recipe for scrumptious maple twists, which immediately became a family favorite. Anneliese and her husband hosted us for meals over thirty years ago when we were both newlyweds. Now she joyfully shared her blueberry scone recipe. Betty, a dedicated commenter, sent me her summer fruit roll recipe. What I soon realized was that here was a treasure of talent waiting to be unwrapped, and so the idea to create a blog dedicated to showcase recipes from our Mennonite/Russian heritage was born.

Kathy, a dear friend for over thirty years, chose to be part of the fun. We were neighbors, had children the same age, and shared countless suppers at each other's home. Kathy's friend Bev, who is gifted in hospitality, was also invited to share the recipes that she enjoyed. My dear cousin, Julie, who loves to write, became a natural addition. Her keen desire was to create gluten-free recipes that were just as tasty as any wheat product. Ellen, already a seasoned blogger, became our "adopted American cousin." Of the cooks, she is the only non-Canadian, but we do share a common heritage in that our parents and grandparents were born in Russia and came to North America as immigrants.

In this book we have featured Mennonite/Russian heritage recipes in honor of the women who taught us the joy of cooking and serving. Over the years, we have come to appreciate the stories and history behind these recipes, stories our grandparents were hesitant to share because of painful memories. We have learned that no matter where our people have settled, they have always considered themselves to be Dutch or German, since that is where their ethnic roots lie. Due to persecution in the 1700s, a large number of German Mennonites settled in the Ukraine, where they continued to teach and practice their language and faith. This added a twist of Ukrainian/Russian flavor to the names of some recipes. In the early 1900s, when Mennonites began to experience extreme difficulties, they decided to emigrate to either North or South America. It is these ethnic roots, common love for cooking, and our faith that brought us together.

We Sure Can Cook

Someone once commented, "You Mennonite girls sure can cook," and though I smiled at her generalization of our cooking abilities and heritage, the name stuck. And so we created a blog called *Mennonite Girls Can Cook*. We opened our overstuffed recipe boxes and carefully

documented the traditional recipes that our Mennonite grandmothers had memorized or sometimes just quickly jotted down without accurate measurements or detailed methods. We snapped pictures before setting the food on the table. We shared tactics of plating one serving to capture with our cameras. We downloaded the pictures onto our computers. We added memories and recipes as we published them to the blog. Then, with great anticipation, we checked the comments that came in, our friends and families graciously developing a tolerance for our constant food talk.

We received emails and comments as a result of our blog, and became aware of the many emotions and memories evoked by the photos and stories from our past.

Bread for the Journey

Our vision for what could be began with a few grains of yeast, was fed by a dash of sugar as excitement, and was watered by the joy of the Lord, who is the Creator of everything good. When we realized that all ten of us shared a common faith in Jesus Christ, we decided to set aside our regular Sunday postings and replace them with inspirational writings, which we named "Bread for the Journey."

Though it is recipes for food that we share, we acknowledge that Jesus Christ is our inspiration to share the joy of hospitality. He is the one who instilled the dream within us to care for those who are hungry. From the very beginning, with our first published post, we agreed that any financial benefit through sponsorship or a "someday book" would all be donated to a cause that feeds hungry children. We humbly offer God our five loaves and two fish, firmly believing that God can produce much from our ordinary talents.

The Cookbook Project

When Herald Press approached us to write this book, the answer was an easy, swift, "yes." We had prayed that God would guide, not only our newly found friendships, but also our future endeavors. This has been a fun, rewarding project for us. We have been blessed with a common goal in which we can share our dreams and passions as sisters of the heart, knowing that God has formed us together as a group for God's purpose.

During the spring and summer, as we began to create this book, we encountered the ups and downs common in every kitchen. If a dish tasted terrific but did not look attractive, it failed to be called "done." When the recipes plated beautifully but needed tweaking in flavor or consistency, it was sent back to the redo list. We groaned with Judy when she had to remake her white bread recipe because she lost the flour count. When she had issues with her raspberry pie photo shoot, and the raspberry crop was finished, we cheered when she found pictures from an earlier shoot. We carefully scrutinized and re-plated comfort foods. We knew they tasted delicious; hastily retrieved bits of garnish from the garden usually did the trick when we had not given much thought to their visual appeal.

Though we attempt to be multi-tasking cooks, recipe writers, plating artists, and photographers, we acknowledge the occasional help from little sous chefs who provided us with much-needed distractions. Our guests didn't mind being beckoned to eat yet another dish for the book. I smiled whenever I saw them looking at the list on my fridge to see what would be the next recipe to taste.

While we worked on the book, we continued to keep recipes fresh on the blog. We hosted summer guests, went camping with our grandchildren, and waited for new grands to arrive. We planned our first summit, had a book contract signing party, and pondered what we would share in our personal stories.

When we realized we would all be together for our contract signing party, we called on a photographer to capture the once-in-a-lifetime moment. Much appreciation goes to Beatriz Photography for the photos, for which we smiled and have since made us smile.

One of the lovely surprises that came our way was in the form of an offer from Kay Dusheck of Ridge Road Indexing in Iowa. When Kay realized that the royalties were being given to charity, she graciously offered to donate her work. Thanks so much for your generous and capable service.

Our Hopes

Since you hold this book in your hand, you have become a partner in realizing our dream that fewer children will go to bed hungry tonight. We hope and pray that, as you leaf through the book and tackle a recipe or two, you too will find joy in sharing the gift of hospitality with those you love.

—Lovella Schellenberg
Abbotsford, British Columbia

Acknowledgments

ANNELIESE FRIESEN: I wish to thank my husband, Herb, who has gratefully acknowledged every meal I've ever made, for his encouragement and patience when the camera accompanies us to the table. I'm thankful to our grandchildren, who keep reminding me about the goodness of buns and jam, and to our children who have smiled through my long ramblings about "the cookbook," also showing much appreciation for the food made by their *Omas*. I am grateful for women who have passed on their love for serving: my mother-in-law and my mom, from whom I am still learning. Most of all I owe a debt of gratitude to God, who has given me so much joy in this stage of my life.

BETTY REIMER: I want to thank my mother, who taught me the love of cooking, and my husband, John, for his wholehearted support and his patience waiting at the table while I photographed the food. Thanks to my children and grandchildren who are always encouraging and willing to sample my recipes. To God be the glory.

BEV KLASSEN: I would like to acknowledge and thank all those who have encouraged me in my love of cooking: my *Omas* and aunts who shared their recipes with me; my mother who loved to entertain and taught me by example; my mother-in-law who lovingly showed me how to make the tops stay on my *Zwieback*; my children and their spouses with whom I regularly exchange recipes; our grandchildren whose faces light up when Nana passes the cookie jar; our friends whose fellowship makes the food taste better; and most of all, my husband, Harv, who daily encourages me in all my endeavors.

CHARLOTTE PENNER: I want to thank my mother and all my aunts who have exemplified generosity and hospitality. Colleen, my sweet friend, thank you for cheering from the sidelines, and for your help with your artistic eye in photographing the food. A special thanks to Tony, Amy, Richard, Jeremy, and Emily for your love

and support, and for being patient as you learned not to eat until after the pictures where taken.

ELLEN BAYLES: I would like to acknowledge my mother Nadia's faithfulness to her family and friends through her cooking and hospitality. She taught us to not be afraid to cook good food and invite people over to share it. To my sisters who have worked hard in writing out my mother's recipes from Russian to English so we can pass them down to our children and grandchildren, thank you. To my non-Russian husband, Greg, who has embraced the culture I was raised in and has accepted my family and food as his own, and to my children, who love their *Baba's* cooking, you have encouraged me to continue in our traditions.

JUDY WIEBE: My husband, Elmer, deserves special thanks for his unwavering support and encouragement in making this book become a reality, and so does my family who cheered from the sidelines. A big thank-you to my grands who occasionally assisted in the test kitchen, and were more than willing to eat *Rollkuchen, Portzelky*, and peppernuts, in season and out.

JULIE KLASSEN: This may seem like a strange acknowledgment but I have to be thankful for having a condition called celiac, which is an autoimmune genetic disorder involving intolerance of gluten (see page 191). Otherwise, I would not have had the privilege of being part of the wonderful team of women who co-authored this book. I also want to thank my family: my husband, Vic; my daughter, Romay; my son-in-love, Vince; and my perfect granddaughters, Elise and Elora, who have been so supportive and encouraging. With unfailing patience they were my testers, always willing to give praise or criticism. I especially thank Elora, who would either give me thumbs-up or politely encourage me with, "Nanna, you ALMOST have it!" And thank you, Elise, for your patient help in answering my computer questions.

KATHY MCLELLAN: I want to thank my husband Scot, our children, Adrienne, Boyd, Carissa, and Jason, as well as my dear sister Rhoda and my dad for their interest and encouragement as I spent time in the kitchen perfecting my recipes. While I stirred, chopped, and rolled I often thanked God for my mom, who got me started in her kitchen. Scot, it takes a patient man to smile and wait for supper while the cook photographs the food she is about to serve. Thank you for eating meals that had cooled off, and also for all your technical support with the computer. I love you all for supporting and affirming me along the way.

MARG BARTEL: I want to recognize my mother, aunts and grandmothers, who have lived fully, in spite of their difficult challenges. They rose to the calling of cooking meals and creating an atmosphere of hospitality around the family table. Thanks to my walking partner who, through rain or shine, continued to inspire and motivate me while listening to my mutterings. I thank my children for their insightful comments and patience with a non-techie, as they so often had to rescue me. As the recipients of many recipes, their comments helped lighten my load. Together we recognize that we will be cooking for the rest of our lives, so we might as well enjoy it and cook together. I've been extremely well served by my husband, who has pushed me to go the second mile, encouraging and prodding me along the way by clicking photos for me, holding my hazelnut torte while the wind was tugging at the tablecloth, and patiently smiling at me, saying, "It will be worth it all." Thanks to all of you for believing in me.

LOVELLA SCHELLENBERG: It is nearly impossible to find meaningful words to offer my family for supporting me and cheering me on. Terry, my beloved, thank you for standing by your "girl." Daily you show me your love and support. You make me happy every day that we found each other in grade nine English class. Terrence and Stuart, I am grateful for the opportunity to have raised sons. Knowing you are a little proud of me means so much. My daughters-by-love, having girls in the house and accepting me as your other mom has meant more than you'll ever know. Lil' Farm Hand, Grandgirlie, Kanneloni Macaroni, and Little Miss Muffet, my darling grands, thank you for being the most endearing food testers ever. Mom, if I could have handpicked my mom by love, I would have still chosen you. Thanks for sharing with me your love of homemaking. I am so thankful to God for his vast love, for giving me a purpose for living, and for assuring me that my end goal is worth looking forward to with joy.

WE WANT TO THANK our girlfriends who listen to us and encourage us, and our wonderful, encouraging blog readers, who keep us fed with heartfelt notes and kind words. Having you along on this journey makes all the difference. You have given us a reason to be published and we applaud you for seeking healthy and economic ways to feed your families.

We wish to thank Herald Press for sending us that first email wondering if we had ever thought about publishing a book. You had no idea that you were part of God's plan for our dream and we are so grateful for the immense support. It has been a joy to work with Amy Gingerich, our editorial director. We appreciate her standard for excellence as well as her guidance and enthusiasm for this project. Thanks to Reuben Graham for seeing our vision and using his design expertise to create a layout that is eye candy to home cooks.

Breakfast and Coffee Break

Farmer Sausage Quiche

Serves 4

- **5 large eggs**
- **½ cup / 125 ml milk**
- **1¼ cup / 310 ml frozen cubed hash browns**
- **1 cup / 250 ml cheddar, mozzarella, and Monterey Jack cheese, mixed and shredded**
- **1 cup / 250 ml farmer sausage (or ham), cooked and cubed**
- **½ cup / 125 ml red pepper, chopped**
- **½ cup / 125 ml green pepper, chopped**
- **¼ cup / 60 ml onion greens, chopped**
- **Salt and pepper to taste**

1. Preheat oven to 350° F / 175° C.
2. In a bowl, whisk milk and eggs.
3. Add all other ingredients.
4. Pour into well-greased 8 x 8-inch / 20 x 20-cm baking pan.
5. Bake for 30 to 40 minutes or until knife inserted comes out clean.

TIP: Prepare this recipe the night before. Cover and refrigerate. Bake uncovered in the morning.

—*Betty*

Kartoffelpuffer
(Potato Pancakes)

Serves 6

- 6 large potatoes
- ½ onion
- 1 teaspoon / 5 ml salt
- Pepper to taste

- 1 cup / 250 ml all-purpose flour
- 2 teaspoons / 10 ml baking powder
- 2 eggs

1. Peel and grate the potatoes.
2. Grate the onion into the potato.
3. Add remaining ingredients and mix well.
4. Shape them into patties.
5. Fry with a little oil in a cast iron frying pan or non-stick skillet.

TIP: Serve with sour cream, ketchup, or applesauce. They are good on their own or served as a side dish with your favorite smoked sausage.

—Charlotte

Eggs Benedict
Serves 4

- 4 English muffins
- 8 eggs
- 8 round slices of ham or back bacon
- Hollandaise sauce (recipe follows)

1. Bring a large pot of water to a boil, and then reduce the heat to a gentle simmer.
2. One at a time, break the eggs and slip them into the water.
3. Gently simmer the eggs for 3–5 minutes, or until whites are firm; remove using a slotted spoon.
4. Toast the muffins, topping one half of each with a slice of ham.
5. Place an egg on top of the ham.
6. Pour a little sauce over the egg. Serve immediately.

Hollandaise Sauce

- 3 egg yolks
- 2 tablespoons / 30 ml lemon juice
- Pinch of cayenne pepper
- Salt and freshly ground pepper to taste
- ½ cup / 125 ml butter, melted and bubbling hot

1. In a blender, mix the egg yolks, lemon juice, and seasoning.
2. With the blender running on very low speed, slowly add the butter; with cover on, blend a little longer until sauce thickens.
3. Spoon sauce over the eggs. Serve extra sauce on the side.

TIPS:

- To reduce all the fuss that can come with making Eggs Benedict, poach the eggs in advance for 3 minutes and chill rapidly by putting them into ice water. They can be refrigerated in the cold water up to 2 days. To reheat, immerse in simmering water for 1–2 minutes.
- If making a large quantity, toast muffins using the broiler setting on your oven.
- Serve with steamed asparagus and a fresh fruit salad.

—*Charlotte*

This has been a Boxing Day tradition for many years. The brunch crowd keeps getting bigger. I have used as many as five dozen eggs and two dozen English muffins to feed my large crowd. Even the pickiest eaters have more than two helpings. Enjoy, then go for a long walk!

Charlotte says

WHAT IF

God is not in the "what if" but the "what is."

Do you find yourself "what if-ing"?
What if I lose my job?
What if I get cancer?
What if the state of the world gets worse?
What if that person doesn't like me?
The what if-ing could go on and on, but it often isn't real; it's just our worried thoughts.

The Bible offers a wonderful formula to get "what if" thinking under control and give you peace again. It gives us assurance, instruction, and a promise.

Let your gentleness be evident to all.
The Lord is near.
Do not be anxious about anything, but in everything,
*   by prayer and petition, with thanksgiving, present your requests to God.*
And the peace of God, which transcends all understanding,
*   will guard your hearts and your minds in Christ Jesus.*
Finally, brothers and sisters, whatever is true, whatever is noble, whatever is right,
*   whatever is pure, whatever is lovely, whatever is admirable—*
*   if anything is excellent or praiseworthy—think about such things.*
Whatever you have learned or received or heard from me, or seen in me—
*   put it into practice. And the God of peace will be with you.* **—PHILIPPIANS 4:5-9 (*NIV*)**

When we are rejoicing, praying, thanking, and thinking on good things, it leaves little room for "what if" thinking. However, the key is to put our faith into practice. When we experience a difficult life situation, there is no "what if" because we have the assurance that God will be with us every step of the way.

May your heart and your mind be guarded and at peace with Jesus.

—Charlotte

Blintzes

Makes 24 Blintzes

- **6 eggs**
- **4 cups / 1 L whole milk**
- **½ teaspoon / 2 ml salt**
- **2 tablespoons / 30 ml sugar**
- **1½ teaspoon / 7 ml vegetable oil**
- **1½ cup / 375 ml flour**

1. Scald the milk. Beat the eggs, then slowly add the milk as you continue to beat.
2. Add the salt, sugar, and oil, beating until blended.
3. Slowly add the flour, beating until combined. Set aside.
4. Use a 10-inch / 25-cm heavy non-stick skillet to cook the *Blintzes*. Heat the skillet; coat it lightly and evenly with vegetable oil. If necessary, coat it again during the cooking process. For a uniform size, use a ⅓ cup / 75 ml measuring cup to dip into the prepared batter. Pour batter onto heated frying pan and swirl the pan to coat the bottom evenly.
5. Cook to golden brown. With a spatula, loosen the edges, flip and brown the other side. Remove from skillet and let cool on a tea towel.
6. Repeat the process until the batter is used up.

Cheese Filling

- **8 ounces / 250 ml ricotta cheese**
- **1 egg**
- **1–2 tablespoons / 15–30 ml sugar**
- **½ cup / 125 ml butter**
- **8 ounces / 250 ml light cream (half and half)**

1. Beat the first 3 ingredients until smooth. Spread about 1 tablespoon / 15 ml filling onto one side of each *Blintz*.
2. Roll up the *Blintzes* and place in a 9 x 13-inch / 22 x 33-cm baking dish. They can be layered.
3. After filling the baking dish, melt the butter and pour evenly over the *Blintzes*.
4. Bake at 350° F / 175° C until heated through, about 10 minutes.
5. Warm the cream. Pour cream over *Blintzes* to cover slightly. You may not need the full amount. Continue baking until the liquid around the *Blintzes* begins to bubble, about 20 minutes.
6. Remove from oven and serve with sour cream, preserves, or syrup.

TIPS:

- You can substitute cottage cheese, hoop cheese, or farmer's cheese for ricotta cheese.
- Experiment with the temperature of the skillet, since it affects the batter. Start with medium temperature.
- When *Blintzes* are cooled, stack them for serving or freeze them.
- To speed up the cooking process, use two skillets.

—Ellen

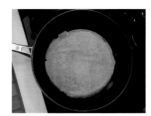
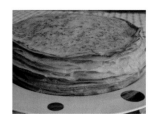

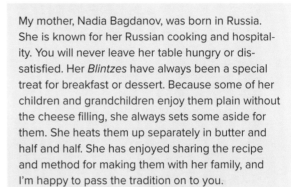

My mother, Nadia Bagdanov, was born in Russia. She is known for her Russian cooking and hospitality. You will never leave her table hungry or dissatisfied. Her *Blintzes* have always been a special treat for breakfast or dessert. Because some of her children and grandchildren enjoy them plain without the cheese filling, she always sets some aside for them. She heats them up separately in butter and half and half. She has enjoyed sharing the recipe and method for making them with her family, and I'm happy to pass the tradition on to you.

Ellen says

This is a favorite egg recipe that is quick and easy, more of an idea than a recipe. All you need is a muffin tin, ham and eggs, and a wee bit of grated cheese along with herbs of your choice.

Judy says

Ham and Egg Cups

Yields 12 portions

- **12 slices deli ham**
- **12 eggs**
- **Grated cheese (cheddar or Parmesan)**

- **Salt and pepper**
- **Fresh basil, chopped**

1. Spray muffin tins with non-stick spray.
2. Line each cup with a slice of deli ham.
3. Gently break an egg into each ham cup.
4. Season with salt and pepper. Sprinkle with grated cheese.
5. Top with chopped basil (or chives or herbs of choice).
6. Bake at 350° F / 175° C for 18–20 minutes.
7. Remove from pan and serve immediately.

TIP: Serve with a fruit salad, hash-brown potatoes, croissants or toast, and call it brunch!

—*Judy*

Who's Cooking

Ellen's Story

My connection with the *Mennonite Girls Can Cook* blog began a generation ago. My parents, Moisi and Nadia Bagdanov, were born in Russia. Both their families escaped from Russia to Iran in the early 1930s. Moisi and Nadia met and were married in Iran. Shortly after World War II, they immigrated to the United States and settled in the Los Angeles area with their many Russian friends and relatives. My mother, who never worked outside the home, cared for her eight children and successfully mastered and documented recipes for the foods from her childhood. Now, her children and grandchildren are enjoying these recipes passed down from her Russian heritage.

My Russian heritage has always been important to me, but even more important has been my spiritual heritage. Growing up, our entertainment and relationships centered on God and food. Meals in our home began with a prayer of thanksgiving. When we had company around the table, the meals generally ended with good hearty praise songs to God. When my extended family gathers for holidays and celebrations, we always sing together.

When I started a blog in 2007, I came across some of the Mennonite gals who were blogging. Soon we realized that many of our recipes were similar. I was graciously adopted and became a contributor to the *Mennonite Girls Can Cook* blog (MGCC). It has been wonderful to get to know my Mennonite friends and learn about their traditions and heritage. Our heritages have a lot in common, both in our cooking traditions and in our faith in God.

The plain pancakes or crêpes have been a family favorite for generations. When I was in elementary school we lived across the street from the school, which made it easy for me to come home for lunch. I enjoyed pancakes made by our Omi, who lived with us. I remember imagining how wonderful it would be if all the students could line up at a window of our home and enjoy these, too . . . for a price, of course.

Our favorite way to eat these pancakes is to sprinkle sugar over the whole pancake, fold it over, and roll it up.

Anneliese says

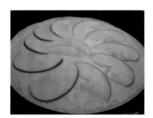

German Pancakes

Yields 12 medium-sized pancakes

- 3 large eggs
- 2¼ cups / 560 ml milk
- ½ teaspoon / 2 ml salt
- 1½ cup / 375 ml flour

1. Preheat medium-sized skillet to medium-low heat. Brush the pan with a small amount of butter for each pancake.
2. Using a hand mixer, beat eggs and milk; add salt and flour until the mixture is smooth.
3. Lift skillet from the heat. Pour ¼ cup / 60 ml batter into the pan, tilting and rotating it until the bottom is covered.
4. Set the skillet back on the heat, cooking until set.
5. Flip over and continue cooking until a golden color.
6. Stack on a plate until ready to serve.

TIP: Serve with cottage cheese and fruit, or use any savory filling of your choice.

Dutch Apple Pancake Variation

- 1 large apple, thinly sliced
- 1 German pancake recipe

Follow the German pancake recipe up to instruction 3.

4. Cover the batter with a single layer of very thin apple slices.
5. Cover the apple slices with another ¼ cup / 60 ml batter.
6. Cook on medium-low until set, not shiny; then flip carefully and quickly.
7. Cook until golden and transfer to a serving plate. Stack until ready to serve. Enjoy these with a mixture of cinnamon and sugar, or syrup.

—Anneliese

Apple Pancakes

Serves 4

- 2 cups / 500 ml flour
- 1 teaspoon / 5 ml salt
- 3 teaspoons / 15 ml baking powder
- ¼ teaspoon / 1 ml cinnamon
- 1 cup / 250 ml coarsely grated apple
- 2 eggs, beaten
- 2 cups / 500 ml milk
- 1 tablespoon / 15 ml butter, melted

1. Mix dry ingredients then stir in the apple.
2. Combine eggs, milk, and butter.
3. Add dry ingredients and stir until combined.
4. Pour ⅓ cup batter onto a lightly greased hot griddle or skillet. Cook until bubbles form on the surface; turn and brown on the other side.
5. Serve with hot apple cinnamon sauce (recipe follows) and whipped cream.

Hot Apple Cinnamon Sauce

- 1 cup / 250 ml brown sugar
- ¾ cup / 175 ml apple juice
- ¼ teaspoon / 1 ml cinnamon
- 1 cup / 250 ml grated apple
- ¼ cup / 60 ml butter

1. Combine sugar, juice, and cinnamon.
2. Boil over medium heat for about 5 minutes, until it has the consistency of heavy syrup.
3. Stir in apple and butter; cook for 1–2 more minutes.

TIP: Add a slice of grilled farmer sausage, and call it a meal!

—Judy

Arme Ritter (French Toast)

Serves 6

- **½ cup / 125 ml flour**
- **2 tablespoons / 30 ml sugar**
- **½ teaspoon / 2 ml salt**
- **2 cups / 500 ml milk**

- **6 large eggs**
- **¼ cup / 60 ml butter**
- **1 loaf bread, thickly sliced**

1. Blend all ingredients except butter and bread, mixing until a smooth, thin batter forms.
2. Pour the thin batter into a large flat-bottomed bowl.
3. Dip bread slices into the batter one at a time; turn them over, and let sit until the batter is absorbed through the bread.
4. Fry slices in a buttered heavy skillet over medium heat until browned well on both sides.
5. Transfer slices to a large ovenproof tray and keep warm in the oven at 250° F / 120° C until ready to serve.

—Lovella

Arme Ritter, or French toast as we call it today, was a staple in many Mennonite homes. By the end of the week the bread was beginning to become stale; this was an excellent way to use it up before the next bread baking day. My mom always added flour to the batter to make the French toast fluffy.

Lovella says

Waffles with Vanilla Custard

Yields 5 deep style Belgian waffles

- 1½ cup / 375 ml flour
- ½ teaspoon / 2 ml salt
- 1 tablespoon / 15 ml baking powder
- 1 teaspoon / 5 ml baking soda
- 1 egg
- 2 egg whites (save yolks for sauce)
- 1¾ cup / 425 ml buttermilk
- 5 tablespoons / 75 ml oil

1. Preheat waffle iron. If you wipe the non-stick surface with an oily paper towel before cooking the first waffle, it should be fine for many subsequent uses.
2. Mix dry ingredients in a medium bowl.
3. Add buttermilk, oil and eggs; mix until smooth using a hand mixer. Let rest for a minute; do not stir before or between scooping batter.
4. Spread a rounded ½ cup / 125 ml batter onto hot waffle iron, leaving room around the edges for the batter to spread.
5. When the waffles are cooked, place them on a wire rack in the oven at 175° F / 80° C to keep warm.

Vanilla Sauce / Custard

- 2½ cups / 625 ml milk, divided
- 4 tablespoons / 60 ml flour
- 2 tablespoons / 30 ml sugar
- ⅛ teaspoon / .5 ml vanilla powder
  or 1 tsp. / 5 ml vanilla extract
- 2 egg yolks

1. In a small pot, heat 2 cups / 500 ml milk over medium heat until it begins to boil.
2. In the meantime, in a small bowl, mix dry ingredients with ¼ cup / 60 ml milk. Blend in the egg yolks, and then the remaining milk.
3. When skin begins to form on the milk, stir in the sauce using a whisk. Continue to stir until the mixture comes to a boil and thickens.
4. Serve warm with waffles.

—Anneliese

Our favorite way to serve waffles is to drizzle homemade freezer raspberry syrup over the custard. I buy half a flat of raspberries when they're in season, put them through the blender, then measure them into a large bowl. For each blended cup of berries mix in 1 cup / 250 ml sugar, stirring for about 5 minutes before letting the mixture set for a few hours. Then stir it again and pour into small jars to freeze. Thaw the syrup just before serving. It keeps a week or two in the refrigerator.

Anneliese says

Pluckets

Serves 8

- **3 eggs**
- **1 cup / 250 ml milk**
- **⅓ cup / 75 ml butter**
- **½ cup / 125 ml sugar**
- **½ teaspoon / 2 ml salt**
- **¼ cup / 60 ml lukewarm water**
- **1 tablespoon / 15 ml instant yeast**
- **4½ cups / 1000 ml flour, approximately**

1. In a large-sized bowl beat eggs well.
2. Scald milk; then add butter, sugar, salt, and water. Let cool to lukewarm.
3. Add liquids to well-beaten eggs.
4. Add the yeast and just enough flour to make a very stiff batter. It will be sticky.
5. Cover and let rise in a warm place until doubled in bulk. Punch down and let rise again.

Dipping Ingredients

- **¾ cup / 175 ml sugar, white or brown**
- **3 teaspoons / 15 ml cinnamon**
- **½ cup / 125 ml chopped nuts (pecans or walnuts)**
- **¼ cup / 60 ml butter**

1. While dough is rising, mix sugar, cinnamon, and nuts. Set aside.
2. Melt butter. Set aside.

Preparing Pluckets

1. When dough has risen the second time, gently punch down. Grease your hands with butter, then pluck and roll or squeeze walnut-sized pieces of dough into balls
2. Dip the balls in melted butter and then roll in the sugar/cinnamon mixture.
3. Pile loosely in an ungreased 1 piece angel food or bundt cake pan. Put any leftover dipping mixture on top of the pluckets. Let the dough rise again for 25–30 minutes.
4. Bake at 350° F / 175° C for 35 minutes. Immediately flip pan upside down onto a plate. Wait a few moments before removing the pan.
5. Serve warm.

TIP: You could use any sweet or plain bun dough for pluckets. I prefer the light texture of this dough.

—Betty

This recipe is known by a several names, such as monkey bread or pull-aparts, but my favorite name for them is pluckets! This would be a perfect addition to a brunch. Wouldn't it be fun to let your guests "pluck at it"?

Betty says

Granola

Yields 12 cups

- 5 cups / 1125 ml quick oats
- ½ cup / 125 ml sesame seeds
- ½ cup / 125 ml pumpkin seeds
- 1 cup / 250 ml unsweetened medium coconut
- 1 cup / 250 ml sunflower seeds
- 1 cup / 250 ml almonds, coarsely chopped
- 1 cup / 250 ml cashews, coarsely chopped
- 2 teaspoons / 10 ml almond flavor
- ¼ cup / 60 ml water
- ¼ cup / 60 ml vegetable oil
- ¾ cup / 175 ml honey

1. Mix first 7 ingredients in a large stainless steel bowl. You may substitute walnuts, pecans, or hazelnuts for the almonds and cashews.
2. In a small bowl, mix the next 4 ingredients, stirring to a smooth consistency.
3. Mix together the wet and dry ingredients, stirring until moistened.
4. Bake in a 9 x 13-inch / 22 x 33-cm baking pan at 350° F / 175° C for 30 minutes, stirring every 3 minutes while it bakes.
5. When cool, put in bags and freeze. Serve over yogurt and fresh berries.

TIP: Stir up a bowl of yogurt, top with some fresh raspberries and a scoop of granola; then enjoy a quick snack filled with nutritious fiber.

—Marg

Healthy living becomes important as we face so many choices. This wholesome healthy recipe comes from one of our family members. I started making this granola a few years ago, and it has become one of the staples in our home. My little grandson uses the word "crumbs" for granola. "Oma, can I have crumbs?"

Marg says

Who's Cooking

Marg's Story

I knew it was the most important moment of my life as I reached for the baton being passed to me. This was no ordinary race; it was the race of my life. Tears pooled in my eyes as my mom looked on, knowing the simplicity of her gift. I was to carry this baton for her as her race neared its end. I felt the cold wood in my hand, and as I slowly turned it over, the words I found engraved on it stopped me in my tracks: "Marg, keep on running with your eyes fixed on Jesus. Mom."

This was her legacy, which would guide me throughout my life's journey. As a young girl, I remember waking up, getting dressed for school, and chasing the cows down the long gravel road to my grandparents' farm. I would sit at the breakfast table eating a large bowl of porridge sprinkled with brown sugar. Grandma would braid my hair, read a Bible verse, and send me off to school. At the end of the day, I would return to Grandma's, eat my snack of fresh fruit or homemade cookies, and chase the cows back home. As a young girl, I saw where my mother's legacy had developed, a legacy that valued the family table, nutrition, hard work, and Bible reading.

In 1973, I married the love of my life. I enjoyed helping my husband pursue his dreams in agriculture. Much of my energy and passion went into giving my three children opportunities to work and play outdoors. Thirty-seven years later, our family is still hiking, cycling, skiing, swimming, and camping together.

Over the years, I have learned the value of running the race. My mother engraved on her baton a clear call to make exercise and diet a priority: "Keep on running . . ." My father's words still echo the old hymn: "Work, for the night is coming." When our daily work was completed, we welcomed the darkness, for this was our time to play sports: baseball in summer, football in fall, and basketball in the hayloft throughout the winter months. I love driving past my homestead looking at the basketball hoop still hanging loosely on the barn wall.

I am passionate about balancing my love for fine foods with consistent exercise and activities. Staying fit does not mean joining the gym; there are many ways to increase your levels of physical activity and integrate them into your life. Even better, choose to do physical activities with your family and friends. They can help you stay motivated.

The baton, which now accompanies me on my journey of life, exemplifies my passions for fitness, food, relationships, and above all, Jesus Christ. It's my prayer that, as I chase my little grandchildren around and watch my adult children on their own journeys, I will be able to hand a baton off to them, leaving them with a legacy, just like my mom did.

Apple *Streusel* Muffins

Yields 12 muffins

- 1 cup / 250 ml flour
- ½ cup / 125 ml whole wheat flour
- ½ cup / 125 ml sugar
- 1 tablespoon / 15 ml baking powder
- 1 teaspoon / 5 ml salt
- ¾ cup / 175 ml butter
- 2 medium apples, chopped, skin on
- 2 cups / 500 ml raisin bran cereal
- 3 teaspoons / 15 ml cinnamon, divided
- 2 eggs
- 1 cup / 250 ml milk
- 2 tablespoons / 30 ml sugar

1. Sift together flour, sugar, baking powder, and salt.
2. Cut in butter with pastry cutter until mixture resembles coarse meal. Set aside ¼ cup / 60 ml.
3. Add chopped apple, cereal, and cinnamon. Mix well.
4. Combine eggs and milk and add to apple mixture, stirring lightly, just until moist. Batter will be lumpy.
5. Fill 12 greased muffin cups and top with the crumbs set aside earlier. Sprinkle with sugar.
6. Bake at 400° F / 205° C for 18–20 minutes or until toothpick comes out clean.

—Charlotte

Imagine waking up to the aroma of freshly baked apples and cinnamon with a faint scent of freshly brewed coffee in the air and the sound of birds singing in the distance. Sounds enticing, doesn't it? Well, you can create this kind of morning for your family or guests. Put the coffee on and let's get baking!

Charlotte says

Blueberry Crumble Muffins

Yields 12 muffins

- ½ cup / 125 ml margarine, room temperature
- 1 cup / 250 ml white sugar
- 2 large eggs
- 1 teaspoon / 5 ml vanilla
- 2 cups / 500 ml flour
- 2 teaspoons / 10 ml baking powder
- ½ teaspoon / 2 ml salt
- ½ cup / 125 ml buttermilk
- 2 cups / 500 ml blueberries, fresh or frozen

1. Beat margarine until fluffy. Add sugar, eggs and vanilla, beating after each addition until creamy.
2. In a separate bowl, mix dry ingredients.
3. Add dry ingredients alternately with buttermilk; stirring until well mixed.
4. Fold in blueberries.
5. Fill well-greased muffin tins almost to the top. Sprinkle crumb topping (recipe follows) on top of the batter.
6. Bake in 375° F / 190° C oven for 20–25 minutes.
7. Cool before removing from tins.

Crumb topping

- ½ cup / 125 ml flour
- ¼ cup / 60 ml sugar
- ¼ cup / 60 ml margarine

1. Stir together flour and sugar; cut in margarine to make fine crumbs.

—Kathy

Warm blueberry muffins with crunchy crumble topping bake up for a perfect coffee time treat. Buttermilk is the key to the soft, moist texture of these muffins.

Kathy says

Rhubarb Orange Sticky Muffins

Yields 16 medium-sized muffins

Muffin Topping

- 1 cup / 250 ml brown sugar
- ¼ cup / 60 ml butter or margarine, melted
- 2 tablespoons / 30 ml whipping cream
- 45–60 pecan halves

1. Grease muffin tins.
2. Mix sugar, butter, and cream together. Using a teaspoon, distribute the topping evenly over the bottom of 16 muffin cups. Add 3 or 4 pecan halves to each cup.
3. Prepare muffin batter.

Muffins

- 2 cups / 500 ml flour
- ¾ cup / 175 ml sugar
- 1½ teaspoon / 7 ml baking powder
- ½ teaspoon / 2 ml baking soda
- 1 teaspoon / 5 ml salt
- 1 large egg
- ¼ cup / 60 ml vegetable oil
- ¾ cup / 175 ml orange juice
- 2 teaspoons / 10 ml orange zest
- 1¼ cup / 310 ml fresh or frozen rhubarb, chopped

1. In a large bowl, combine all dry ingredients.
2. In medium bowl, beat egg. Add oil, orange juice, and zest.
3. Add liquid mixture to dry mixture all at once, stirring until moistened; fold in the rhubarb.
4. Spoon batter over brown sugar/pecan mixture in muffin pans.
5. Bake at 350° F / 175° C for 25–30 minutes.
6. Remove from oven, loosen sides of muffins and turn upside down on a rack.

My friend Betti makes these wonderful muffins. One day I tried adding a sticky pecan mixture to the bottom of the muffin cups before spooning in the batter and now I make them like this each spring during rhubarb season.

Bev says

TIP: These muffins are best served the same day. Store leftovers in the refrigerator. They will still be good the next day, but will be softer in texture. To make the muffins without the brown sugar/pecan topping, add ¾ cup / 175 ml chopped pecans to the muffin batter.

—Bev

I have made these bite-sized delectable rolls many times. Often I am asked for the recipe. The rolls taste especially good when hot out of the oven and dripping with glaze. A delicious coffee break treat!

Betty says

Apple Rolls

Yields approximately 30 rolls

- **2 cups / 500 ml flour**
- **4 teaspoons / 20 ml baking powder**
- **1 teaspoon / 5 ml salt**
- **¾ cup / 175 ml shortening**
- **½ cup / 125 ml sour cream**
- **½ cup / 125 ml buttermilk**
- **3–4 apples**

1. Mix dry ingredients in a bowl; cut in shortening until size of peas.
2. Add sour cream and buttermilk, stirring with fork until dough forms into a ball and can be handled easily.
3. Cover dough and refrigerate for 1–2 hours.
4. Roll out dough to the same thickness as a pie and cut into squares.
5. Peel and core the apples and cut into eighths.
6. Place a slice of apple diagonally in the center of each square piece of dough.
7. Bring up 2 corners of the dough and pinch together on top.
8. Bake at 400° F / 205° C for 16 minutes or until golden in color.

Glaze

- **1 cup / 250 ml icing sugar**
- **½ teaspoon / 2 ml vanilla**
- **4 teaspoons / 20 ml warm water**

1. Mix and brush on the apple rolls while still warm.

—*Betty*

Blueberry Scones

Yields 12 scones

- 2 cups / 500 ml flour
- ¼ cup / 60 ml sugar
- 1 tablespoon / 15 ml baking powder
- ½ teaspoon / 2 ml baking soda
- ¼ teaspoon / 1 ml salt
- 1 teaspoon / 5 ml vanilla
- 1 tablespoon / 15 ml orange or lemon zest
- ¼ cup / 60 ml butter
- 1 cup / 250 ml buttermilk
- 1 egg
- 1–2 cups / 250–500 ml blueberries

1. Mix dry ingredients in medium bowl.
2. With pastry blender, cut butter into dry ingredients until fine.
3. Mix liquid ingredients in a small bowl; add to dry ingredients. Fold in blueberries.
4. Drop by large tablespoons onto parchment-lined baking pans.
5. Bake at 400° F / 205° C for 20–22 minutes, depending on size.
6. Drizzle with glaze while still warm.

Glaze

- ¾ cup / 175 ml icing sugar
- 2 tablespoons / 30 ml orange juice
- 1 teaspoon / 5 ml lemon or orange zest

1. Mix to spreading consistency.

TIP: To freeze blueberries: rinse to remove debris, spread out on paper towel-lined cookie sheets to dry and then fill large plastic containers and place in freezer.

—Anneliese

As a child, I reluctantly went berry-picking in the summer to make some spending money, but now I find it relaxing to get out there among the rows and rows of berries, especially when I am with good company. Not only do I enjoy the outdoors, but also I can anticipate the berry desserts to come.

Anneliese says

Bread
FOR THE
Journey

DON'T FORGET

When you have eaten and are satisfied, praise the Lord your God for the good land he has given you. Be careful that you do not forget the Lord your God, failing to observe his commands, his laws and his decrees that I am giving you this day. —DEUTERONOMY 8:10-11 (*NIV*)

Although these are God's words to the people of Israel, I can't help but think how they apply to me. After losing her husband and two children in Russia, my grandmother fled to Germany with one young son, my father. He told us how he had to look for food in trash cans. It's no wonder he would never allow us to complain at the table. If we fussed or found fault with the meal, it was just cause to send us away from the table. He knew both the pain of hunger and the blessing of having a table before him filled with food.

Today, we live in a land of plenty, boasting flowing wheat fields, wineries, orchards, dairy, and poultry farms. The city where I live happens to be one of the berry capitals of the world. No matter the season, we can find almost any ingredient to make delicious meals, snacks, and desserts. Yes, we have much more than we need.

I want to remember to give thanks, giving heed, lest I forget that it is the Lord God who gives.

—Anneliese

Berry-Filled Scones

Yields 12 scones

- 2 cups / 500 ml flour
- 1 tablespoon / 15 ml sugar
- 1 tablespoon / 15 ml baking powder
- ½ teaspoon / 2 ml salt
- ½ cup / 125 ml butter, cubed
- 1 cup / 250 ml whipping cream
- 1 teaspoon / 5 ml vinegar
- ½ teaspoon / 2 ml baking soda
- ½ cup / 125 ml sour cream

- 2 cups / 500 ml berries, such as strawberries, blueberries, raspberries, blackberries, or a combination
- 2 tablespoons / 30 ml sugar for sprinkling
- 1 egg, beaten with 1 tablespoon / 15 ml milk

Glaze

- 1 cup / 250 ml icing sugar
- 1 tablespoon / 15 ml warm water

1. Combine the flour, sugar, baking powder, and salt in a large bowl. Using your fingers, rub in the butter to make small crumbs.
2. Stir the vinegar into the whipping cream.
3. In a small bowl, mix baking soda with sour cream.
4. Combine the wet and dry ingredients; knead the dough gently for 30 seconds until a soft dough forms.
5. Roll out the dough to ¼-inch / .63-cm thick on a floured surface. Use a large round drinking glass to cut out round shapes.
6. Place half the rounds on a cookie sheet covered with parchment paper.
7. Arrange berries in the center of each round; sprinkle lightly with sugar.
8. Cut small circles from the center of the remaining rounds of dough.
9. Top each scone with the pieces of dough that have the centers removed; press the edges together with the tines of a fork.
10. Brush the scones with the egg/milk mixture.
11. Bake in a 400° F / 205° C oven for 20 minutes or until golden brown.
12. Make a thin glaze by mixing the icing sugar with warm water; drizzle over the berry scones as soon as you remove them from the oven.

TIP: Pat the dough into a circle and score into eight triangles and then bake until golden brown to make delicious plain scones that taste wonderful when served with Devonshire cream or crème fraîche and lemon curd (see page 137 for a lemon curd recipe).

—Lovella

The scone dough recipe originates with my friend Sally's mother. I have been tucking fresh berries into the scones each summer and can never really decide whether it is breakfast or coffee break or even dessert. Add a scoop of ice cream if in doubt.

Lovella says

Lemon Poppy Seed Loaf

Yields 1 loaf

- **3 egg whites**
- **1¾ cup / 425 ml flour**
- **1 teaspoon / 5 ml baking soda**
- **½ teaspoon / 2 ml baking powder**
- **2 tablespoons / 30 ml poppy seeds**
- **2 tablespoons / 30 ml lemon zest**
- **⅔ cup / 150 ml sugar**
- **⅓ cup / 75 ml oil**
- **⅓ cup / 75 ml applesauce**
- **¼ cup / 60 ml lemon juice (from 2 lemons)**
- **¾ cup / 175 ml sour cream**

Glaze

- **½ cup / 125 ml icing sugar**
- **1 tablespoon / 15 ml lemon juice**

1. Beat egg whites until soft peaks form and set aside.
2. In a large bowl mix flour, baking soda, baking powder, poppy seeds, and lemon zest.
3. In a medium bowl combine sugar, oil, and applesauce; whisk in lemon juice.
4. Stir this mixture into the flour mixture alternately with the sour cream.
5. Fold in beaten egg whites.
6. Pour into a greased 9 x 5-inch / 23 x 12-cm loaf pan.
7. Bake at 350° F / 175° C for 45–50 minutes or until toothpick inserted comes out clean.
8. Cool in pan for 10 minutes before removing to rack. Mix the glaze and pour over loaf.
9. Cool, slice and serve!

—Betty

Date Loaf

Yields 2 loaves

- ½ pound / 250 g pitted dates, chopped
- 2 cups / 500 ml brown sugar
- 2 cups / 500 ml boiling water
- 2 teaspoons / 10 ml baking soda
- 2 eggs
- 3 cups / 750 ml flour
- ½ teaspoon / 2 ml salt
- 1 teaspoon / 5 ml vanilla

1. Place chopped dates and brown sugar in a large glass or metal mixing bowl.
2. Pour boiling water over date mixture.
3. Add baking soda and stir well until the foaming stops. Let stand for 15 minutes.
4. Beat eggs and combine dry ingredients; add both to date mixture.
5. Pour into 2 greased loaf pans.
6. Bake at 325° F / 175° C for 50–60 minutes, or until toothpick inserted comes out clean.
7. Let stand for 5 minutes before removing to a cooling rack. Freezes well.

—Kathy

Warm date loaf smothered in butter brings back memories of stopping by my mom's place for coffee and a visit. The softened dates are what give this dense loaf its moistness and rich taste.

Kathy says

Soups, Salads, and Sides

I often double or triple the noodle recipe and layer the strips of dough on top of each other and slice through all the strips of dough to make ½-inch / 1-cm noodles. Simply boil the noodles in a large pot of salted water and serve with *Schmaundt* fat (recipe on page 86) and fried onions.

Lovella says

Butter Soup

Serves 6

- 8 cups / 2 L water
- 1½ teaspoon salt
- 1 large onion, chopped
- 6 medium fresh potatoes, diced
- 1 large bay leaf
- 5 whole cloves
- 8 peppercorns
- 1 star anise
- Handful of fresh parsley

1. Bring water to boil. Add salt, onion and potatoes and simmer for 15 minutes.
2. Tie the spices, except for parsley, into a square piece of cheesecloth and add to the soup.
3. Let simmer while you make the noodles.
4. Add the chopped parsley to the soup and simmer another 15 minutes.

Noodles

- 1 large farm fresh egg
- 2 tablespoons / 30 ml water
- 1 cup / 250 ml flour
- ½ teaspoon / 2 ml salt

1. Stir together the egg, water, and salt. Stir in half the flour, turn it onto a floured surface, and knead in the rest of the flour. You may need a little more flour to make the dough firm.
2. Roll out the dough. Cut 2-inch / 5-cm strips across the length of the dough.
3. Dust excess flour off the noodle dough; using a clean pair of kitchen scissors, cut ½-inch / 1-cm noodles directly over the pot, into the soup.
4. Boil several minutes until the noodles float.
5. Ladle it into bowls, and add a dollop of butter and a bit of cream.

—Lovella

When my beloved began coming over for dinner when we were dating, my mom would make this soup for him. I often think that this soup secured the eventual proposal of marriage. I still make it for him when I want to serve him something special.

I really don't know why it is called butter soup. The dollop of butter and the bit of cream added at the table give the flavor that makes you want more.

Lovella says

Chicken Noodle Soup

Serves 8

- 1 chicken or 8 chicken thighs (with bone)
- 2 bay leaves
- 10 peppercorns
- 1 star anise
- 5 cloves
- Small handful parsley, chopped
- 1 chicken bouillon cube
- 1 teaspoon / 5 ml salt
- 12 cups / 125 ml water

1. Place chicken in a soup pot; cover with the water and bring to a boil.
2. Tie the spices, except for the parsley, into a small piece of cheesecloth and add to the soup.
3. Simmer 2–3 hours.
4. Remove from heat; remove chicken from the bones when cool enough to handle.
5. If you have used a whole chicken, remove the breasts and refrigerate for another use.
6. Add the remaining meat from the bones to the broth.
7. Add the salt, bouillon cube, and parsley.
8. Simmer for ½ hour, taste and adjust the salt if needed.
9. Serve the broth over cooked fine egg noodles.

Fine Egg Noodles

- 2 eggs
- 2 tablespoons / 30 ml water
- 2 cups / 500 ml flour, approximately
- 1 teaspoon / 5 ml salt

1. In a medium bowl, beat the eggs with the water. Add flour and salt, stirring well.
2. Turn dough out onto a floured surface. Knead until the dough rolls easily and does not stick to the surface.
3. Roll out very thinly and cut into 2-inch / 5-cm wide strips or use a hand-cranked pasta roller to create fine noodles.
4. Dust liberally with flour and stack the strips; then cut through all the layers to form very thin noodles.
5. Scatter the noodles on a floured surface to dry.
6. Bring a large pot of water to boil; add 1 tablespoon / 15 ml salt. Cook the noodles just a few minutes, until they float to the surface.
7. Strain the noodles in a colander and serve with the hot broth.

TIP: Do not store leftover soup with noodles, as the noodles will continue to swell in the broth.

—*Lovella*

My mom often made this chicken noodle soup for Sunday lunch. She would leave the broth simmering gently on the stove. When we walked in the house after church, the fragrance welcomed us in the door. The Russian Mennonite version of chicken noodle soup did not include vegetables; the noodles were piled in the bowl and then covered with broth.

Lovella says

Green Bean Soup

Serves 8

- 1 pound / 500 g smoked ham hock
- ½ dried red hot pepper
- 10 black peppercorns
- 1 bay leaf
- 1½ teaspoon / 7 ml salt
- 1 large onion, chopped
- 2–3 carrots, chopped
- 2 medium potatoes, cubed
- 6 cups / 1400 ml chopped green beans (frozen or fresh)
- Small handful summer savory
- 1 bouillon cube (chicken or beef) if needed, for extra flavor
- ½ cup / 125 ml sweet or sour cream

1. Cover ham bone with about 8 cups / 2 L water in large pot.
2. Tie spices into cheesecloth and add to pot.
3. Bring to a boil, skim off the scum, and simmer about 1 hour.
4. Remove the bone; add vegetables, and cook for another hour.
5. While vegetables are cooking and after ham has cooled slightly, remove the meat from the bone, chop it into bite-sized pieces, and return it to the pot.
6. About 30 minutes before serving add summer savory, tied together for easy removal, and bouillon if needed for flavor.
7. Just before serving, add sweet or sour cream.

—Anneliese

This *Gruene Bohnen Suppe* brings back memories of my childhood. At that time it was not one of my favorites, but when I made it for my collection, I was pleasantly surprised! The sweet cream transformed the flavor to taste like one of my favorite soups served at a local Italian restaurant. Maybe it was the memory, or perhaps I finally acquired a taste for it. It's the perfect soup to make with a leftover ham-bone.

Anneliese says

Split Pea Soup

Serves 8

- 12 cups / 2.5 L cold water
- 1½ cup / 375 ml dried, split peas (yellow or green)
- ½ cup / 125 ml baby lima beans, navy beans or pot barley
- 1 teaspoon / 5 ml salt
- ½ package / 20 g dry onion soup mix (optional)
- 2 chicken bouillon cubes (if not using ham hock)
- 1 bay leaf
- 10 whole black peppercorns
- ½ dried red hot pepper
- 1 small ham hock (1 pound / 500 gm), 6 European wieners, or half a farmer sausage
- 1 onion, chopped
- ½ green or red pepper, chopped
- 3 carrots, sliced
- 2 small potatoes, diced
- 2 tablespoons / 30 ml summer savory

This was a favorite soup when our kids were growing up. They liked it with sliced European wieners.

Anneliese says

1. Begin by putting water, rinsed peas, beans or barley, salt, and spices into a large pot.
2. If using a ham hock, add it at this time, omitting the bouillon cubes.
3. Bring the uncovered pot to a boil. Use a slotted spoon to remove the scum from the surface. Cover, reduce heat, and simmer for 1–1½ hours. Keep lid open a crack during the cooking time.
4. Remove the ham and allow it to cool while you prepare and add the vegetables. If not using ham, add wieners or cut up sausage and bouillon cubes at this time.
5. Remove ham from the bone; add it to the pot along with summer savory.
6. Simmer for another hour until done, stirring/scraping occasionally to prevent the cooked peas from settling at the bottom and burning.

TIP: When reheating the soup, frequently scrape the bottom of the pot with a flat utensil. If the soup gets too thick, just add a little water.

—Anneliese

Cabbage *Borscht* (Soup)

Serves 8

The Ukrainians made *Borsch*, and the Mennonites of the Ukraine borrowed the soup recipe, substituting cabbage as the main ingredient rather than beets, and called it *Borscht*. At our home, *Borscht* was not an appetizer, but a thick and hearty soup that was eaten as the main meal. It was always served with white bread, fresh from the oven. With potatoes, carrots, cabbage, and dill in the garden and soup bones in the freezer, *Borscht* was easy to prepare and inexpensive, accounting for the term, "cheap like *Borscht*." Then and now *Borscht* continues to be an inexpensive, substantial meal.

Judy says

- 2 pounds / 1 kg beef soup bone, with lots of meat
- 8 cups / 2 L water
- 2–4 carrots, sliced
- 4 medium potatoes, cubed
- 1 large (or 2 medium) onions, chopped
- 1 medium head cabbage, chopped fine
- 2 teaspoons / 10 ml salt
- ¼ teaspoon / 1 ml black pepper
- 2 whole red chili peppers (dried)
- Fresh dill, a handful or to taste
- 2 - 10 ounce / 284 ml cans tomato soup
- 2 cups / 500 ml tomatoes, diced (optional)

1. Cover soup bones with water and simmer for several hours until meat is tender.
2. Remove the bone and shred the meat.
3. Add more water to measure a total of 8–10 cups stock.
4. Add vegetables and seasonings. Place chili peppers and dill into a spice holder or cheesecloth. Cook until vegetables are tender.
5. Add tomato soup, diced tomatoes, and shredded beef; bring to a boil.
6. Serve with sour cream.

TIP: Fresh dill works the best in this recipe. Dill can also be harvested in season and stored in zip-close plastic bags in the freezer.

—Judy

Bread
FOR THE
Journey

LOVE WORTH SAVORING

Taste and see that the Lord is good; blessed is the one who takes refuge in him.
—PSALM 34:8 (*NIV*)

As I wandered through my garden I was drawn to the pot filled with different herbs that I use for cooking. I thought about each herb and how it adds the right flavors to the food I cook. Each one contributes its own distinctive flavor and brings out the best taste of the food.

I think about God and the richness I find in savoring and enjoying each morsel in his Word. These morsels speak to me of love, joy, hope, peace, and forgiveness. They are the "herbs of my soul," the qualities I want to cultivate and allow God to use to his glory.

I am reminded not to rush as I read the Bible, but to let my mind absorb God's goodness and allow it to nourish my soul. God's love is worth savoring.

—Betty

Cauliflower Cheese Soup

Serves 4

- 1 large head cauliflower, cut into small florets
- 1 carrot, grated
- 1 stalk celery, chopped
- 3 cups / 750 ml chicken broth
- ¼ cup / 60 ml butter or margarine
- 1 small onion, chopped
- ¼ cup / 60 ml flour
- ½ teaspoon / 2 ml salt
- ⅛ teaspoon / .5 ml black pepper
- 2 cups / 500 ml milk
- 1 cup / 250 ml cheddar cheese, grated
- Parsley or chives (optional)

1. Cook cauliflower, carrot, and celery in chicken broth until tender. Do not drain.
2. Mash vegetables with a potato masher.
3. Melt butter in large saucepan. Add onion and sauté until limp. Do not brown.
4. Blend in flour, salt, and pepper. Add milk. Heat and stir until it boils and thickens.
5. Add cheese and stir until cheese melts.
6. Add this sauce to mashed cauliflower mixture. Remove from heat and serve.
7. Garnish with parsley or chopped chives, if desired.

—Judy

Savory Cheddar Scones

Yields 8 scones

- 3 cups / 750 ml flour
- 2 tablespoons / 30 ml baking powder
- ¾ teaspoon / 3 ml salt
- ⅓ cup / 75 ml butter
- 1 cup / 250 ml buttermilk

- 2 eggs
- 1 cup / 250 ml cheddar cheese, coarsely grated
- 1 teaspoon / 5 ml dill weed
- 1 tablespoon / 15 ml chives, finely snipped

1. Preheat oven to 400° F / 205° C. If using a cast-iron skillet, preheat and grease pan.
2. Combine flour, baking powder, and salt. Cut in butter to form pea-sized pieces.
3. Add grated cheddar and herbs.
4. Mix eggs and buttermilk, and quickly add them to the flour mixture. Combine until just blended.
5. Move the dough to a well-floured surface and knead a few times.
6. Pat into a circle about 1-inch / 2.5-cm thick.
7. Cut into 8 wedges and place on a parchment lined baking sheet or in a cast-iron skillet.
8. Bake in preheated oven for 20–25 minutes or until golden.

TIP: The key to light and fluffy scones is to handle the dough as little as possible. If you don't have buttermilk on hand, replace it with 1 cup / 250 ml whole milk and 1 teaspoon / 5 ml lemon juice.

Pop the extra scones into the freezer. Reheat to serve "fresh" scones tomorrow or another tomorrow.

—Judy

Quick and easy and so much fun to serve from a cast iron skillet! I form the dough into a circle to fit my 12-inch / 30-cm cast iron skillet.

Judy says

My family loves this zesty soup especially on a cold day.

Betty says

Taco Soup

Serves 4

- **1 pound / 500 g lean ground beef**
- **½ cup / 125 ml onion, finely chopped**
- **1 cup / 250 ml celery, finely chopped**
- **14 ounce / 398 ml can tomato sauce**
- **12 ounce / 341 ml can corn, with liquid**
- **14 ounce / 398 ml can kidney beans, drained**

- **⅓ cup / 75 ml salsa**
- **1 tablespoon / 15 ml chili powder**
- **3 tablespoons / 45 ml taco seasoning**
- **3 cups / 750 ml water**
- **Taco chips**
- **Cheese, shredded**
- **Sour cream**

1. Cook beef, onion, and celery until meat is browned, and onion and celery are tender.
2. Add the rest of the ingredients; simmer for 15 minutes.
3. Add taco chips, shredded cheese, and sour cream to individual soup bowls.

—Betty

Our community is famous for its sweet smelling country air and Chilliwack corn. From early July until well into fall we enjoy the best sweet corn around. An added bonus is being able to pick it fresh right on our farm.

This soup is best cooked in season, using fresh corn and vegetables right from the garden. It became a family favorite over the years and was always served at our family camp. A rich, hearty soup with a wonderful aroma, it freezes well and really hits the spot after a long day of skiing.

Marg says

Corn Chowder

Serves 10

- 4 cups / 1000 ml potatoes, cubed
- 2 cups / 500 ml carrots, sliced
- 2 cups / 500 ml celery stalks, sliced
- 2 medium onions
- 2 green peppers
- 1 pound / 500 g bacon or substitute 1½ pound / 750 g farmer sausage (approximately 1 ring), cut into bite-sized pieces

- 2 - 10 ounce / 284 ml cans creamed corn (or 4 large fresh cobs)
- 2 - 10 ounce / 284 ml cans cream of celery soup
- 2 - 10 ounce / 284 ml cans cream of mushroom soup
- 2 quarts / 2 L milk
- ½ teaspoon / 2 ml crushed red pepper

1. Cook potatoes, carrots, and celery together in a small amount of water. Drain.
2. Sauté onions, green peppers, and meat.
3. Place meat, vegetables, and remaining ingredients into large soup pot. If using fresh corn, cook and remove kernels. Heat slowly as milk tends to scorch easily. Stir often.

TIP: Reheat the chowder in the microwave to prevent scorching.

—*Marg*

Sunday is meant to be a day of rest, a practice that was observed much more in my grandparents' day than it is today. The women would prepare the Sunday meal on Saturday. In our home it was often a meal of ham or farmer sausage, fried potatoes or potato salad, and some type of fruit moos, with either a clear or cream base. This was made with fresh fruit in season and dried fruit in the winter.

Obst Moos is not considered a "poor man's" dish anymore, especially with the cost of dried fruit today. In the Russian Mennonite tradition, Obst Moos was served at every celebration, such as Christmas, Easter, and Pentecost. It was even served at weddings.

Charlotte says

Obst Moos (Cold Fruit Soup)

Serves 10

- 8 cups / 2 L water
- 3 cups / 750 ml mixed dried fruit, such as apples, apricots, pears, prunes, cherries, raisins
- 1 box (⅓ cup / 75 ml) cherry-flavored gelatin
- ¾ cup / 175 ml sugar
- 4 tablespoons / 60 ml cornstarch
- 1 can or jar of sour cherries with liquid (any size)

1. Put water in large pot.
2. Add any combination of dried fruits.
3. Bring to a boil. Simmer until done, about 15–20 minutes.
4. Meanwhile, combine the gelatin, sugar, and cornstarch.
5. Add to the fruit and cook an additional 3–4 minutes, until thickened.
6. Cool and store in the refrigerator.
7. Enjoy this as a cold summer soup or serve over ice cream, cold vanilla pudding or cream of wheat pudding.

—*Charlotte*

Coleslaw Dressing

Yields enough for 2–3 pounds / 1000–1500 g of shredded cabbage/carrot mix

- ½ cup / 125 ml sugar
- 1½ tablespoon / 20 ml flour
- 1½ teaspoon / 7 ml dry mustard
- 1 teaspoon / 5 ml salt

- 1 egg
- ⅓ cup / 75 ml vinegar
- ½ cup / 125 ml water
- 1 cup / 250 ml sour cream

1. In a small pot, mix dry ingredients.
2. Add egg and stir well.
3. Stir in vinegar and water. Bring to boil, stirring constantly. Cool.
4. Mix with 1 cup / 250 ml regular or light sour cream. Refrigerate until needed.

TIP: To the cabbage, add chopped apples and/or raisins, and sprinkle with sunflower seeds. This recipe will serve about 20 when served with other salads. I often cook half the recipe (still using the whole egg) for our family.

—Anneliese

> This recipe was used before my mom had access to bottled dressings. I have not found a dressing I like as much as this one.
>
> *Anneliese says*

Santa Fe Chicken Salad

Serves 4

- 4 chicken breasts, boneless and skinless
- Chili powder or Cajun seasoning
- 8 cups / 2 L mixed salad greens
- 1 - 14 ounce / 398 ml can black beans, drained and rinsed
- ¾ cup / 175 ml corn kernels (fresh off the cob or canned)
- Red onion, several slices, chopped
- 2 avocados, halved and sliced
- ½ cup / 125 ml feta cheese
- ¼ cup / 60 ml roasted peanuts, chopped
- Fried tortilla strips or crushed tortilla chips

Peanut Lime Vinaigrette Dressing
- ½ cup / 125 ml lime juice (about 3 limes, juiced)
- ½ cup / 125 ml olive oil
- 1 tablespoon / 15 ml peanut butter
- 2 teaspoons / 10 ml Dijon mustard
- 3 tablespoons / 45 ml lime zest
- ¼ cup / 60 ml dry roasted peanuts, finely chopped

1. Prepare the salad dressing. Using a blender, mix lime juice, olive oil, peanut butter, and mustard. Blend until emulsified. Stir in lime zest and finely chopped peanuts.
2. Prepare the salad ingredients in separate containers.
3. Grill chicken breasts rubbed with seasoning. Let the chicken breasts rest for several minutes; slice in strips before adding to salad.
4. To serve, assemble the salad on 4 plates.
5. Start with a bed of greens; sprinkle with sliced onions, beans, and corn.
6. Top each with a grilled chicken breast, half an avocado, crumbled feta cheese, peanuts and tortilla strips.
7. Drizzle with dressing and serve.

TIP: To prepare tortilla strips, cut four tortillas into strips ¼-inch / .5-cm wide and several inches long. Fry on medium-high heat until golden. Drain on paper towels. These can be prepared a day ahead.

—Judy

Broccoli Salad

Serves 6

- 2 bunches raw broccoli, cut in small chunks
- 1 medium onion, diced
- ½ cup / 125 ml raisins
- ¾ cup / 175 ml mayonnaise
- ⅓ cup / 75 ml sugar
- 2 tablespoons / 30 ml vinegar
- 8 slices crisply cooked bacon, cut in small pieces
- 2 tablespoons roasted sunflower seeds

1. Mix mayonnaise, sugar, and vinegar and blend well.
2. Mix broccoli, onion, raisins, and half of the bacon in a bowl.
3. Pour mayonnaise mixture over the broccoli mixture, mix well and cover.
- Refrigerate for several hours.
- Just before serving, stir in the remaining bacon and the sunflower seeds.

—*Betty*

This is a delicious make-ahead salad to serve at any meal. It's a simple and easy dish to prepare for a potluck.

Betty says

Who's Cooking

Betty's Story

I grew up on a farm in the small Rosengard school district. As a young girl, I was taught to cook, clean the house, and do laundry, all important household jobs to learn. I was also taught to respect people no matter who they were or from what walk of life.

I believe this prepared me for the direction of my life's path. My parents were very hospitable; many friends and family would drop by for visits. I remember visiting one family who had a child with special needs. I was a little afraid of her, but soon realized that she just wanted to join us and be part of the fun. Even at that young age, I noticed the love and acceptance her family had for her.

I grew up, married, and had my own family, two beautiful daughters and then a beautiful son. At the age of seven months, our son was diagnosed with tuberous sclerosis and later with autism as well. We were not given much hope that he would ever walk, speak, or function normally. We would have to deal with seizures, mood swings, anger, and other behavioral problems. However, with much help and perseverance, he learned to crawl and then walk, and began to string words together. Then, for a week, he suffered multiple seizures and lost all speech. One day alone, I counted thirty-five seizures.

At our next visit to the pediatrician, I hoped for encouraging words from him and more help for us. Instead, we were advised to put our son in an institution because, he said, it would just be too hard for us to raise him. We left the doctor's office deeply disappointed in his advice but knowing that God would be with us on our journey. Not once did we consider our pediatrician's advice. Later, our daughter told us that our decision had been very reassuring to her young mind. She was afraid that if we couldn't keep our son at home maybe we couldn't keep her either.

Our son is now thirty-five years old and, although there have been many challenges and rough patches in the journey, we have been blessed beyond measure. God has given us the ability to care for our son, to have hope, and to love him for the gift that he is. God has assured me that my son's soul is whole and that his body is only temporary.

I have often thought of the child that I met many years ago and remember that children like her just want to be loved and accepted as they are.

There are many verses from scripture that I have found encouraging. One of my favorites is this: "My grace is sufficient for you, for my power is made perfect in weakness" (2 Corinthians 12:9a; NIV).

God is good!

Potato Salad

Serves 10 as a side dish

- 6 large fresh red or white potatoes to make 6 cups / 1.5 L when cooked
- 10 hard boiled eggs, peeled
- ¼ cup / 60 ml green onions, finely chopped
- 1 cup / 250 ml salad dressing or mayonnaise
- ½ cup / 125 ml sour cream
- 2 tablespoons / 30 ml pickles, sweet or dill, finely chopped (optional)
- 2 tablespoons / 30 ml pickle juice, sweet or dill
- 1 teaspoon / 5 ml salt
- ¼ teaspoon / 1 ml pepper

1. Boil potatoes with skins in a large pot of boiling salted water for 25 minutes or until tender.
2. Peel the potatoes with a sharp knife while they are still quite warm; cool completely.
3. Using a sharp paring knife and a cutting board, cut the potatoes in half, and then cube them to make uniform pieces.
4. Chop the eggs, and add with onions to the potatoes.
5. Combine the remaining ingredients and pour over the salad. Mix well.
6. Chill an hour before serving.

TIP: It is easy to adjust the ingredients to make a larger salad.

—Lovella

There are several different types of "Mennonite" potato salad. Some prefer it on the sweet side and some add vinegar in the dressing for tang. My mom-in-law, Pauline, is always requested to bring her potato salad to family gatherings. My kids love it because she takes the time to cut her potatoes in small even cubes.

Lovella says

Carrot Salad

Serves 10–12

- 2 pounds / 1 kg carrots
- 1 medium onion
- 1 small green pepper
- 2 stalks celery
- ¾ cup /175 ml vinegar
- 1 teaspoon / 5 ml Worcestershire sauce
- ⅓ cup / 75 ml sugar
- ½ teaspoon / 2 ml dry mustard
- ½ teaspoon / 2 ml salt
- ½ teaspoon / 2 ml pepper
- ½ cup / 125 ml vegetable oil
- 1 - 10 ounce / 284 ml can tomato soup

1. Peel and slice carrots. Cook until tender crisp.
2. Slice onion, celery, and pepper into thin slices or rings; add to cooked carrots. Set aside.
3. Bring the remaining ingredients to a boil. Pour this mixture over the vegetables.
4. Cool and stir occasionally.
5. Store in a covered container in refrigerator.

—Kathy

The Sunday school church picnic was a highlight for me. It was the one Sunday we could wear pants to church. I remember my dad planning the music for the outdoor service, and my mom packing up her picnic basket with the items she had signed up to bring for the potluck lunch.

Families all traveled to the church camp where excited children piled out of cars. We ran to find our friends and soon gathered on the lawn for the morning service. The women of the church brought an abundance of salads, meats, buns, and desserts. The church family would usually sing the doxology, "Praise God from Whom all Blessings Flow" before the meal.

After lunch, the games began. There was no such thing as being a spectator; even our parents jumped into gunnysacks and hopped to the finish line. My dad could run like the wind in his day. I remember being so proud as he crossed the finish line. We would join in the balloon toss, three-legged race, and then came the grand finale, the tug-of-war. When the games were over we were treated to small ice cream cups with their little wooden spoons. Those were the days; we thought they would never end.

This carrot salad recipe is just one of the ones I remember from church potlucks. It keeps for at least a month, making it a great salad to have on hand for summer picnics.

Kathy says

Leafy Lettuce Salad

Serves 6

- 8 cups / 2 L leafy garden lettuce
- ½ cup / 125 ml sugar
- ½ cup / 125 ml cream
- ½ cup / 125 ml vinegar

1. Blend the sugar and cream together; add vinegar.
2. Pour over the leafy lettuce and serve.

—Marg

I remember this salad from my childhood. My mother's monthly grocery budget was a mere $50. With that she fed her family of seven as well as all the farm hands. She had a gift of hospitality, and knew how to stretch her pennies. Actually, she always asked God how she could make her budget last. She worked hard and always had a garden. I asked my sister for Mom's secret leafy lettuce salad recipe. So simple, yet so good! Do any of you recall a similar fresh lettuce salad?

Since I am no longer working outside the home, I have made an effort to grow a garden again. I love gardening with my grandkids. This year we built raised garden beds and this has renewed my interest in gardening. From the garden to the table—it's the best way to eat!

Marg says

Bread
FOR THE
Journey

NEVER GIVE UP

But now, this is what the Lord says—he who created you, Jacob, he who formed you, Israel: "Do not fear, for I have redeemed you; I have summoned you by name; you are mine.

When you pass through the waters, I will be with you; and when you pass through the rivers, they will not sweep over you. When you walk through the fire, you will not be burned; the flames will not set you ablaze. For I am the Lord your God, the Holy One of Israel your Savior."
—ISAIAH 43:1-3A (*NIV*)

It was a few years back when someone shared this Scripture with me in such a way that it has never left me. When I put my own name into the verses it becomes a powerful lesson in trusting God. God never promised us an easy way out. Many times, believers think that life will be easy because they have taken a new step of faith.

We know that we will go through difficult times in our lives, but if we invite the Lord to go with us, it will make our load lighter. God did not say that he would keep us from difficult times. When we go through difficult times, we can drown or we can grow stronger. God promises that he will protect us, just as a father cares for his child.

"Do not be afraid, for I am with you." **—ISAIAH 43:5A**

God gives renewed hope to all who are going through difficult situations.

—Marg

Chicken Tarragon Salad

Serves 4 as a main course

- 4 boneless chicken breasts
- 2 green peppers
- 2 red peppers
- 1 red onion
- 2 heads Romaine lettuce
- 1 bunch onion greens, chopped

1. Grill chicken breasts over medium-high heat until done.
2. Cut peppers and red onions into long, thin strips.
3. Cut or tear lettuce into bite-sized pieces.
4. Combine lettuce and vegetables in large salad bowl.
5. Cut cooled chicken into strips and arrange on top of the assembled salad.

Tarragon Dressing

- 2 tablespoons / 30 ml vinegar
- 2 tablespoons / 30 ml fresh tarragon leaves, chopped
- 2 tablespoons / 30 ml lemon juice
- 1 teaspoon / 5 ml Dijon mustard
- ½ teaspoon / 2 ml Worcestershire sauce
- 10 tablespoons / 150 ml olive oil

1. Mix all ingredients with a hand blender.
2. Pour the dressing over the salad.
3. Sprinkle with additional fresh tarragon.

—Marg

Salad time can be anytime at our home! There's nothing like a freshly tossed salad to complement any kind of barbecued meat. Over the past years, since the children have left home, salads have become a staple dish at our place. The flavor of fresh tarragon is what makes this recipe stand out. The chicken breasts can be fried or oven-baked, but we prefer them hot off the grill. This salad is a family favorite, and I often hear the words, "Mom, why don't you make more?"

Marg says

January 4, 2022! ✱✱✱

Steel Head House
Tom v Nik

Greek Lemon Roasted Potatoes

Serves 6

- 6 large potatoes with or without peel, cut into wedges
- 2–4 tablespoons / 30–60 ml olive oil
- ¼ cup / 60 ml lemon juice, freshly squeezed
- 1 tablespoon / 15 ml chicken bouillon, dissolved in a ¼ cup / 60 ml water
- 2 teaspoons / 10 ml dried oregano
- 2 cloves garlic, minced, or garlic powder to taste

1. Peel and cut potatoes.
2. Place in a 9 x 13-inch / 22 x 33-cm baking pan.
3. Combine remaining ingredients together and pour over potatoes, stirring well to coat every piece.
4. Bake at 425° F / 220° C for 1 hour, stirring every 20 minutes.

TIP: Cover potatoes for the first half hour; if you prefer crisp edges, leave uncovered for the entire time. For more intense lemon flavor, sprinkle with additional lemon juice just before serving.

—Charlotte

★★★ January 7, 2022 — poached eggs over top — Nix ✓ Tom

Cheesy Scalloped Potatoes

Serves 6

- 6 large baking potatoes, peeled and thinly sliced
- ½ cup / 125 ml onion, finely grated *Additional*
- 1 cup / 250 ml cheddar cheese, grated
- 2 tablespoons / 30 ml butter
- 2 tablespoons / 30 ml flour
- 1 teaspoon / 5 ml salt
- ½ teaspoon / 2 ml pepper
- 1¾ cup / 425 ml milk

1. Prepare potatoes in a large bowl. Cover with cold water and let stand for 10 minutes to remove some of the starch. Drain well.
2. Add onion and cheese to the potatoes; stir to combine.
3. Melt butter in microwave. Stir in flour, salt, and pepper, blending well.
4. Add milk and microwave for 1 minute. Stir and heat another minute until mixture begins to bubble and thicken.
5. Generously grease a large shallow casserole or glass pan, 9 x 13-inch / 22 x 33-cm. Place potatoes into casserole and pour hot milk mixture over potatoes. The milk should almost cover the potatoes. If needed, add a little extra milk to top it off. There is no need to heat it up first.
6. Bake covered in 350° F / 175° C oven for 40 minutes. Uncover and bake another 15–20 minutes or until potatoes are fork tender.

TIP: Scalloped potatoes are a great side dish to serve with ham or sausage. If you want a meal in one dish, add precooked cubed ham or sausage to the potato mixture before baking.

—Kathy

This is a perfect dish for a potluck dinner.

Kathy says

Glazed Carrots

Serves 4

- 1 pound / 500 g carrots, sliced
- 2 tablespoons / 30 ml butter
- 1 tablespoon / 15 ml fresh lemon juice
- ½ teaspoon / 2 ml garlic salt or powder
- ½ teaspoon / 2 ml dried basil
- Freshly cracked pepper to taste

1. Steam carrots until tender crisp. Strain.
2. Melt butter. Stir in remaining ingredients and toss with the carrots.

TIP: This sauce is great on fresh green beans and other vegetables, giving them a bit of punch.

—*Charlotte*

Sesame Asparagus Stir-fry

Serves 4

- 2 tablespoons / 30 ml sesame oil
- 2 tablespoons / 30 ml sesame seeds
- 2 tablespoons / 30 ml ginger, grated
- 2 tablespoons / 30 ml garlic, minced
- 2 tablespoons / 30 ml shallot (or onion greens), minced
- 4 cups / 1000 ml asparagus, sliced in ½-inch / 1.25-cm pieces
- 1 cup / 250 ml bean sprouts
- 1 cup / 250 ml julienned red or yellow bell peppers
- 2 tablespoons / 30 ml soy sauce
- Juice of 1 lime

1. Heat sesame oil in a skillet or wok until sizzling hot.
2. Quickly add the sesame seeds, ginger, garlic, shallot, and asparagus.
3. Stir-fry for 1 minute.
4. Add bean sprouts and julienned peppers.
5. Continue to stir-fry for another minute or until tender crisp.
6. Remove from heat and add soy sauce and lime juice. Combine well.

—Marg

Our family loves asparagus. In our early years on the dairy farm, we often enjoyed fresh asparagus from our neighbor's garden. To this day, my children love nothing more than melted butter poured over freshly cooked asparagus. This past year I decided to try a new version and here is a recipe that passed my family's inspection. Do not be afraid to introduce something new to your family or friends.

Marg says

Who's Cooking

Kathy's Story

I have fond memories of the train and car trips our family took from British Columbia to Winnipeg, Manitoba, to visit my grandparents.

In my earlier years, those holidays were spent at Grandma and Grandpa Regehr's little farm. It was a novelty to feed the chickens, collect eggs, and run about the farmyard. Inside the farmhouse was a root cellar with a trap door. I loved going down the little set of stairs to help pick a jar of jam or pickles. Grandma usually made our requested favorites: *Wareneki*, cabbage rolls, *Zwieback*, and wonderful apple pies or *Perishky*.

After supper we would gather in their living room. While Grandma crocheted, she and Grandpa would ask us about our lives, and we listened as they told stories of their years in Russia. Though the years were hard, they had such thankful hearts.

Grandma told us how she learned to help others by the example of how others had helped them. When her family moved to Canada they were very poor. Since the train passed by their farm, travelers would come to their door asking for food. She usually had a little something to share with those who had less than her family had. Her love for God, Grandpa, family, and others was evident.

When Scot and I started our family we lived in the same town as my parents. Our girls did not have to travel far to visit their Grandpa and Grandma Janzen. Grandma's house was the next best place to home. Meal times were fun and Grandma's food was the best.

As our girls got older, they spent time having meaningful conversations with my mom, who was gifted in relationship building. She modeled her love and devotion for Jesus, as well as her love and commitment to her husband. The year after both of our daughters married, my mom passed away. Several months later I became a grandma to our only granddaughter. Since then our daughters and sons-in-law have each added two sons to their families.

Being a grandma is the icing on my life. Scot and I are enjoying our five grandchildren, and when they come running in the door for supper, a play day, or extended visit, their warm hugs, smiles, and playful little voices steal my heart. While Grandpa pulls out high chairs and booster seats, I fill sippy cups and tie bibs on the youngest ones. These sweet visits are worth every crumb under the table, toy on the floor, or blanket that needs to be washed. Having these little children to love and spend time with is a gift and privilege that comes with a responsibility: to live my life in a manner that reflects Jesus to them.

Meat Pinwheels

Serves 4

Meat Filling

- 1 pound / 500 g lean ground beef
- 1 small onion, minced
- ½ teaspoon / 2 ml salt
- ½ teaspoon / 2 ml pepper
- 1 - 10 ounce / 284 ml can cream of mushroom soup

1. Cook beef and onions until beef is browned and onions are tender. Drain any grease.
2. Stir in soup, salt and pepper; simmer for 5 minutes.
3. Allow mixture to cool completely while making the biscuit dough.

Biscuit Dough

- 2 cups / 500 ml flour
- 2 tablespoons / 30 ml sugar
- 1 teaspoon / 5 ml salt
- 4 teaspoons / 20 ml baking powder
- ½ teaspoon / 2 ml cream of tartar
- ¼ cup / 60 ml cold butter
- 1 cup / 250 ml milk

1. Stir together the dry ingredients.
2. Cut in butter with a pastry blender until crumbly.
3. Add milk and stir until dough begins to form a ball.
4. On a lightly floured surface, gently knead dough into a smooth ball. Sprinkle more flour on the surface; roll out dough into a ½-inch / 1.25-cm thick rectangle.
5. Spread cooled meat mixture onto the dough and roll up like a jellyroll.
6. Slice 1-inch / 2.5-cm thick slices and place, almost touching, onto parchment lined or greased baking sheet. Makes approximately 12–15 pinwheels.
7. Bake in 425° F / 220° C oven for 15–20 minutes. Meat will bubble and biscuits should be golden brown.
8. Remove from oven and let rest on baking sheet while making the cheese sauce.

Cheese Sauce

- ¼ cup / 60 ml butter
- 2 tablespoons / 30 ml flour
- 1¼ cup / 300 ml milk
- ¼ teaspoon / 1 ml salt
- ¼ teaspoon / 1 ml pepper
- ¾ cup / 175 ml cheddar cheese, grated

1. Melt butter in microwave.
2. Add flour and stir until smooth.
3. Add milk and spices, stir well and place back in microwave for several minutes, until mixture bubbles.
4. Whisk well; microwave another 30 seconds.
5. The mixture should be thick yet pourable. If mixture is too thick add a little milk and heat for another 30 seconds.
6. Add cheese to the hot milk mixture and stir well until all the cheese has melted.

—Kathy

When my mom invited guests for lunch, she would serve these savory pinwheels along with hot cheese sauce. There was usually a crisp garden salad served on the side.

Kathy says

My mother-in-law raised and fed nine children, along with a few extras that came to the table, without using a single recipe book. Often she had to improvise and make do with whatever she had on hand. One of my favorite meals from when I joined the family was *Bubbat*, which she served along with chicken *Borscht* and *Plumimoos* (cold fruit soup) for dessert.

As a newlywed, I attempted to make this recipe, but the words in the Mennonite cookbook threw me for a loop: "Flour to make a stiff dough (then) pour into greased pan." What did that mean?

Much later into my marriage I found out that my mother-in-law had a hand-written recipe in her possession, which she rarely re-ferred to, relying instead on her memory. When I tried making *Bubbat* according to her recipe, I called her up and asked, "Did you put in 4 cups of flour, like it says?" She said, "Put in more if it's not enough." What's not enough? I finally got it out of her that you should be able to stir it with a wooden spoon. So, that's the secret. It all depends how strong your arm is, especially when you decide to quadruple this recipe!

Anneliese says

Bubbat (Bread) **with Farmer Sausage**

Serves 10

- 2 cups / 500 ml milk, scalded
- 1 teaspoon / 5 ml salt
- ¾ cup / 175 ml ice cold water
- 4 eggs
- 5 cups / 1125 ml flour
- 1 tablespoon / 15 ml instant yeast
- 4 cups / 1000 ml chopped farmer sausage and/or smoked ham

1. Scald milk and add salt. Add cold water and cool until warm.
2. Beat eggs well, add warm liquids, and then stir in the flour, 1 cup at a time. Add instant yeast with first cups of flour.
3. Stir in sausage or ham.
4. Spread onto 1 greased 9 x 13-inch / 22 x 33-cm pan and 1 loaf pan, or place it all on an 11 x 17-inch / 8 x 43-cm cookie sheet. Cover with plastic and let rise 1 hour.
5. Bake at 350° F / 175° C for about 45 minutes. If the *Bubbat* is baked in a cookie sheet, reduce the baking time.

—Anneliese

Rührei (Scrambled Eggs)

Serves 2 as a main course

- **6 tablespoons / 90 ml flour**
- **½ cup / 125 ml milk**
- **6 eggs**
- **½ teaspoon / 2 ml salt**
- **1½ tablespoon / 25 ml butter**

1. Mix flour and milk into a smooth paste.
2. Add eggs and salt, mixing into a thin batter.
3. Melt butter in skillet over medium heat.
4. Pour in egg mixture.
5. Cut and turn mixture until completely cooked through and lightly browned.
6. Serve hot.

—*Judy*

In my Mennonite tradition, scrambled eggs were called *Rührei*. This was never a breakfast meal at our place, but rather a quick lunch or supper. This dish is a version of scrambled eggs, a cross between an omelet and a pancake. Some prefer to serve pancake syrup on their *Rührei*, but we like to add a touch of freshly ground pepper and serve it with salsa for a little zip. It pairs well with ham or sausage to make a simply satisfying meal.

Judy says

Suppers

Kotletten were often served on weeknights with boiled potatoes and onion cream gravy, or made ahead to serve cold on Sunday with potato salad. In fact, they were part of the meal at our wedding. My husband still asks for them on a regular basis. They make great picnic food as well.

My mother made her *Kotletten* small, more like a meatball, and deep-fried them in hot oil.

My mother-in-law made hers about 3-inches / 7.5-cm in diameter and about ¾-inch / 2-cm thick like a hamburger patty, frying them in 1–2 tablespoons oil.

Both ways of cooking them are good.

Bev says

Kotletten (Meatballs)

Serves 4–6

- 1 pound / 500 g lean ground beef
- 1 egg
- 1–2 slices day old bread (2 if slices are small)
- 1 potato, peeled and finely grated
- ½ cup / 125 ml milk
- 1 small onion, chopped fine or grated
- 1 teaspoon / 5 ml salt
- ⅛ teaspoon / 0.5 ml pepper
- Fine breadcrumbs (optional)
- Vegetable oil

1. Mix the egg, milk, potato, and onion in a bowl.
2. Tear bread into pieces and soak in liquid until soft.
3. Add ground beef, salt, and pepper and mix well by hand. The mixture should be fairly soft.
4. Form meatballs or patties, rolling each in breadcrumbs if desired.
5. Heat oil in skillet; fry or deep fry until bottom is browned.
6. Turn *Kotletten* over and brown the other side.
7. Keep warm in oven until all are done.

Kotletten Sandwich Recipe Variation

- Leftover *Kotletten*
- ½ medium onion, sliced
- ¼ red or yellow pepper, cut into strips
- ¼ green pepper, cut into strips
- Cheddar cheese and/or mozzarella cheese, grated
- Bread slices
- Butter and barbecue sauce, or mayonnaise (optional)

1. Sauté onion and pepper in a skillet until they lose their crunch. Set aside.
2. Place bread slices on a baking pan and toast lightly in the oven.
3. Turn the slices over and spread other side with butter and barbecue sauce, or use mayonnaise.
4. Cut leftover *Kotletten* in half and lay flat sides on bread. If desired, warm it slightly in a skillet before placing on the bread.
5. Top with sautéed vegetables and grated cheese.
6. Broil, watching closely until cheese melts.
7. Serve open faced with bread and butter pickles.

—Bev

Meatloaf

Serves 6

- 1¼ pound / 625 g lean hamburger
- 1 teaspoon / 5 ml salt
- ¼ teaspoon / 1 ml pepper
- ½ cup / 125 ml dried bread crumbs
- ½ cup / 125 ml rolled oats
- ¼ cup / 60 ml ketchup
- 1–2 teaspoons / 5–10 ml fine dried onion flakes
- 1 cup / 250 ml cheese, grated
- ⅓ cup / 75 ml milk

Topping

- ¼ cup / 60 ml ketchup
- ¼ cup / 60 ml barbecue sauce
- 2 tablespoons / 30 ml brown sugar

1. Prepare a 9 x 13-inch / 22 x 33-cm baking pan by lining it with foil or parchment paper.
2. Mix all ingredients well and shape into loaf.
3. Place the loaf on the baking pan; make an indentation along the top of the loaf.
4. Cover meatloaf completely with topping.
5. Bake at 350° F / 175° C for 60–75 minutes, depending on size and shape of the loaf.

—Anneliese

Holubschi (Cabbage Rolls)

Serves 10

- 1 large head savoy cabbage
- 2 pounds / 1 kg ground beef
- 2 cups / 500 ml cooked whole grain rice
- 1 large onion, finely minced
- 2 large eggs
- 1 teaspoon / 5 ml salt
- ½ teaspoon / 2 ml pepper
- Small handful parsley, finely minced
- 1 tablespoon / 15 ml prepared horseradish (optional)
- 2 cups / 500 ml tomato juice (see tip)
- 2 bay leaves
- 2 - 10 ounce / 284 ml cans tomato soup
- 1 cup / 250 ml whipping cream
- 1 tablespoon / 15 ml maple syrup or brown sugar
- 1 tablespoon / 15 ml balsamic vinegar

TIPS:

- There is plenty of sauce in this recipe to pour over mashed potatoes, if desired.
- If you use two casserole dishes, you will need additional tomato juice to cover all the cabbage rolls.
- Do not cover the *Holubschi* directly with foil, as the acid will break down the foil, leaving little bits on your rolls.
- If you bake them from the freezer, add an additional ½ hour to the baking time.

Holubschi are cabbage rolls. I often make large batches in summer when the cabbage is fresh at the local farm markets. They are easy to assemble, cover in plastic wrap, and freeze.

Lovella says

1. Several days before you plan to serve the *Holubschi*, place the savoy cabbage in a zip-close plastic bag and put it in the freezer for a full day. When ready to prepare the *Holubschi*, remove cabbage from the freezer and thaw in a cool place. This softens the leaves so there is no need to boil the cabbage.

2. Optional cabbage preparation: place the cabbage in a large pot, covering it with water. Bring to a boil and simmer until the leaves are softened and can be removed easily.

3. Mix the ground beef, cooled cooked rice, onion, eggs, salt, pepper, parsley, and horseradish in a large bowl. Use your hands to mix until well combined.

4. Remove the leaves from the core of the cabbage head. Place about 1 cup / 250 ml meat mixture at the base of a cabbage leaf and roll up, tucking in the sides as you roll toward the top of the leaf. Repeat with all the leaves, adjusting the amount of meat mixture to the size of the leaf.

5. Spray a large 4 quart / 4 L casserole with non-stick cooking spray.

6. Arrange the *Holubschi* seam-side down in the pan. Do not layer them; use an additional pan if necessary.

7. Pour over just enough tomato juice to cover the *Holubschi*.

8. Lay the bay leaves in the sauce on top of the *Holubschi*.

9. Cover and bake in the center of a 325° F / 160° C oven for 2 hours.

10. Combine the remaining ingredients and pour over the *Holubschi*. Bake covered for another hour.

—Lovella

Tacos

Yields 6–8 shells

Shell Ingredients
- 1 cup / 250 ml white flour
- ½ cup / 125 ml cornmeal
- 1½ cup / 375 ml water
- 1 egg
- 1 teaspoon / 5 ml salt

Step One, Dry Fry

1. Whisk ingredients together until smooth and runny.
2. Spray a skillet with a small amount of non-stick cooking spray.
3. Place pan over medium heat for 1 minute.
4. Pour ½ cup / 125 ml batter into the middle of the pan, using the back of a spoon to swirl batter into a very thin circle.
5. Allow shell to set; flip and fry the other side.
6. Cool on wire rack.

TIP: You can use the shells immediately, or for added flavor and a slight crispness, continue with step two. The dry shells can be made ahead of time, but the deep-frying should be done just before serving. These do not freeze well.

Step Two, Deep Fry

1. Using a deep-sided skillet, add about 2-inches / 5-cm oil to the pan and heat to medium-high or until it sizzles when a shell is added. If the oil is too hot the shells become too crispy. Test oil temperature by dipping the corner of 1 shell into oil.
2. When oil is the right temperature, drop shells in one at a time and let fry for about 20 seconds. Using a fork and spoon, flip each shell and fry another 20 seconds. Do not over fry because they must be rolled after they are filled.
3. Remove shells to a baking sheet lined with paper towels to absorb excess oil.
4. Keep warm in a low-temperature oven.

> When I was dating my husband we attended a church with a fantastic youth group. His mom often invited a group of young people over for a taco feast. I had never eaten homemade shells, nor had I tried mashed potatoes, peas, or pickles in tacos. I tried it, liked it, and that is how I have served tacos ever since. My sons-in-law love tacos, but they tease me every time they see the strange fillings, saying that if they wanted shepherd's pie they would have asked for it. I just smile and watch them devour taco after taco. You'll never go back to hard shell tacos again after you've tasted these. They are worth the effort.
>
> *Kathy says*

Filling Ingredients
- 1 pound / 500 g hamburger, fried
- 2 cups / 500 ml potatoes, cooked and mashed
- 1 cup / 250 ml peas, cooked
- 2 tomatoes, diced
- 6 dill pickles, diced
- 3 cups / 750 ml lettuce, shredded
- 1 medium onion, diced
- 2 cups / 500 ml cheddar cheese, grated
- Taco sauce or salsa

Instructions

1. Place shell on plate. Place a scoop of potatoes on the shell and spread down the middle.
2. Layer with meat, peas, onions, and remaining chopped vegetables.
3. Add your favorite taco sauce and top it all with grated cheese before rolling up.

TIP: Be creative! Add salt and pepper or a package of taco seasoning to the hamburger when you fry it. Add a small amount of milk and butter to make the potatoes creamy. Or add other ingredients such as sour cream, guacamole, black olives, celery, or refried beans.

—Kathy

HOSPITALITY

Be hospitable to one another without grumbling. —1 PETER 4:9 (*NKJV*)

Do not forget to entertain strangers, for by so doing some have unwittingly entertained angels. —HEBREWS 13:2 (*NKJV*)

Hospitality was taught by example in many Mennonite homes when I was a child. Friends, family, and neighbors knew they were welcome at any time. It was not unusual to invite strangers in for a meal.

The Bible urges each of us to show hospitality to those around us and to do it generously, without complaining. Hospitality is also listed as a spiritual gift, given in a special way to some individuals.

Some people think that hospitality requires a specially set table and/or an elaborate meal. However, in our busy lives, most of us have neither the time nor inclination to do this.

The hospitality the Bible speaks of requires us to share willingly what we have: a bowl of soup, take-out pizza, a cup of coffee, a beautifully prepared meal or a warm bed, the offer of a ride, or a place to stay when misfortune strikes. There are many ways to show hospitality to one another. And don't forget to extend the same hospitality to your children, your parents, and yes, even to yourself. In doing so you are a living example of the grace God has extended to you.

—Bev

Savory Pot Roast with Roasted Vegetables

Serves 6

- 1 tablespoon / 15 ml cooking oil
- 1 (3–4 pound / 1.5–2 kg) pot roast
- Salt
- ¼ cup / 60 ml ketchup
- 2 tablespoons / 30 ml soy sauce
- 2 tablespoons / 30 ml Worcestershire sauce
- ½ teaspoon / 2 ml dry mustard
- 1 teaspoon / 5 ml dried rosemary crushed
- ¼ cup / 60 ml red wine vinegar
- 2 cloves garlic minced
- ¼–½ cup / 60–125 ml water
- 1 tablespoon / 15 ml brown sugar
- 1 tablespoon / 15 ml cornstarch

1. Heat oil in a Dutch oven on top of the stove. Add roast, browning slowly on both sides. Remove from heat.
2. Drain off fat; sprinkle roast with a little salt.
3. Combine all ingredients except for the last 3, and pour over roast. Return to heat.
4. Cover tightly; simmer 1¾–2 hours, or until meat is tender.
5. Transfer meat to serving platter. Loosely cover with foil and let stand while you make the gravy.
6. Skim off excess fat in Dutch oven. Heat pan juices to a slow simmer, scraping down the brown bits with a spatula.
7. Mix cornstarch with water and brown sugar until blended.
8. Pour slowly, a little at a time, into pan juices, stirring constantly, and adding just enough to make the gravy smooth. Bring to a slow boil.
9. Remove from heat. Serve with sliced roast and roasted vegetables.

Roasted Vegetables

- Carrots
- Potatoes
- 2 tablespoons / 30 ml oil
- Kosher salt, as desired
- 1 clove garlic, minced
- Freshly ground pepper

1. Thirty minutes before the meat is done, heat oven to 425 ° F / 220 ° C.
2. Cover a large baking pan with parchment paper.
3. Peel carrots and potatoes; cut into uniform pieces.
4. In a bowl, combine oil, salt, garlic, and pepper.
5. Toss vegetables in oil mixture and lay out on prepared pan.
6. Roast in prepared oven for 15–20 minutes or until vegetables are browned and tender.

TIP: Prepare this recipe in a slow cooker and have a great meal ready for the end of the day.

—Bev

This pot roast's appeal comes from the delicious, full-flavored gravy.

Bev says

Rolled-up *Kielke* (Noodles)
Serves 6

Kielke (Noodles)
- 2½ cups / 600 ml flour
- 2 teaspoons / 10 ml salt
- 2 extra large eggs, measuring ½ cup / 125 ml
- ½ cup / 125 ml milk

1. Stir the eggs, milk, and salt into the flour; knead until dough becomes smooth.
2. Cover and let rest for 30 minutes.
3. Sprinkle flour over the counter; roll the dough thinly enough to see through. This takes time and patience, but it is crucial that the dough is very thin and measures approximately 24 x 16-inches / 60 x 40-cm.

Rolled-up *Kielke* (Noodles)
- ⅓ cup / 75 ml bacon drippings
- 1½ pound farmer sausage
- 8–10 fresh medium sized potatoes, cut each into 8 pieces
- 2 medium onions, diced
- 1 teaspoon / 5 ml salt
- ½ teaspoon / 2 ml pepper
- ½ cup / 125 ml chopped fresh parsley

1. Spread the bacon drippings evenly over the rolled-out noodle dough.
2. Roll up the dough tightly, beginning with the longer side. (This step can be done earlier in the day.)
3. Cut the long roll into 3 equal pieces, wrap in plastic wrap, and refrigerate until you are ready to slice and steam the noodles.
4. Cut the farmer sausage into serving size pieces. Place meat in the bottom of a large heavy pot with a lid.
5. Add potatoes, then the onions. Sprinkle with the salt, pepper, and parsley.
6. Add enough water to barely cover the meat. Bring to a boil.
7. Cover with a heavy lid, turn heat to medium and simmer for 30 minutes.
8. While the sausage, potatoes, and onions are simmering, slice the noodle rolls into ¼-inch / ½-cm lengths.
9. Lift the lid and gently place the noodle rolls on top of the meat and vegetables in the pot. Quickly replace the lid to prevent steam from escaping.
10. Simmer another 30–45 minutes, until most of the liquid is absorbed and the sausage is beginning to sizzle in the pot.
11. Serve with *Schmaundt* Fat / Cream Gravy (recipe follows).

Schmaundt Fat (Cream Gravy)
- ¼ cup butter
- ½ cup heavy cream
- ½ cup sour cream

1. Melt the butter over low heat, add the heavy cream and sour cream and bring to a slight simmer.
2. Serve over rolled-up *Kielke*.

—Lovella

My beloved fondly remembered his Grandma Fast making this for him, and so I asked her for the recipe. She explained the method and I made a batch up for my noodle lover. It took me several tries to get it right. Eventually I wrote it down; now I am documenting it for future generations. The noodles are steamed rather than boiled. They are firm, dense noodles that absorb the flavors of the broth from the sausage, onions, and potatoes. Since farmer sausage is not readily available everywhere, you can use cubed ham or other smoked sausage in the recipe.

Lovella says

Spaetzle aren't really a Mennonite specialty, although they are very similar to *Kielke* (meaning noodles). In Germany, *Spaetzle* are served alongside pork and *schnitzel* dishes. They are wonderful when served plain with butter, but often they are served smothered in mushroom gravy or fried with onions and bacon. For those of us who have to watch our weight, a smaller helping is advised but do try them.

This is a *Spaetzle* maker. Prior to getting it as a gift from my Swiss neighbor, I placed a flat grater over my pot of boiling water and used a spatula to "swipe" the batter over the grater. A colander with large holes works as well; however a *Spaetzle* maker makes it much easier. They are available at many kitchen stores.

Spaetzle (German Dumplings)

Serves 4

- 2 cups / 500 ml flour
- 1 teaspoon / 5 ml salt
- 2 eggs, slightly beaten
- ¾ cup / 175 ml milk
- 3 tablespoons / 45 ml butter

1. Place flour and salt in mixing bowl.
2. Combine eggs and milk; stir into the flour mixture until a sticky batter forms.
3. In a large pot bring to a boil 12 cups of water to which 1 teaspoon / 5 ml salt and 1 teaspoon / 5 ml oil have been added.
4. Place batter by spoonfuls in a *Spaetzle* maker or colander; push batter back and forth, allowing it to fall in small pieces into the boiling water.
5. Occasionally stir *Spaetzle* or add a small amount of vegetable oil to the pot to prevent sticking.
6. Once all the *Spaetzle* are in the water, cook for 1–2 minutes longer.
7. Use a colander to drain the water and return *Spaetzle* to pot. Stir in butter.

TIP: For a tasty option, slowly caramelize a large chopped onion in 1 tablespoon / 15 ml butter over low-medium heat in small skillet. Stir into the *Spaetzle* just before serving.

Another tip is to double the recipe. *Spaetzle* taste very good the next day when fried with bacon and onions, assuming there are any leftovers!

—Bev

Sautéed Red Cabbage

Serves 4–6

- 2 tablespoons / 30 ml olive oil
- 1 small onion, thinly sliced
- ½ medium head red cabbage, shredded
- ¼ cup / 60 ml vinegar
- 2 tablespoons / 30 ml sugar
- 1 teaspoon / 5 ml salt
- ½ teaspoon / 2 ml pepper

1. Sauté onions in olive oil over medium heat for 2–3 minutes. Add cabbage and continue to sauté 5 minutes.
2. Add vinegar, sugar, and seasonings. Lower heat and cook for 10–15 minutes, stirring occasionally.

TIP: Sautéed red cabbage is the perfect side dish to serve with *Wareneki* (recipe on page 90) or *Spaetzle* (recipe on page 88).

—Kathy

Wareneki (Cottage Cheese Pockets)

Serves 4–6

Dough Ingredients

- ½ teaspoon / 2 ml salt
- ½ teaspoon / 2 ml baking powder
- 2 cups / 500 ml flour
- 1 egg white, slightly beaten (save yolk for the filling)
- 1 cup / 250 ml sour cream

Dough Instructions

1. Place dry ingredients into a mixing bowl.
2. Stir in egg white and sour cream.
3. Using your hands, knead until the dough is smooth. Cover and refrigerate for 1 hour.
4. While the dough is chilling, make the fillings (recipes follow). Each filling recipe is enough for 1 recipe of dough.
5. On a lightly floured surface, roll 1 recipe of dough into a very thin rectangle.
6. Using a small ice cream scoop, place balls of filling along one end of dough.
7. Fold dough over filling. Use a small round cutter to press down over each mound of filling. The dough is very easy to work with and should stick together. If it doesn't, pinch the edges to seal in the filling.
8. Place *Wareneki* on a parchment-lined baking sheet and refrigerate until ready to boil, or freeze them on the sheet until solid. Store them in freezer bags.

Cottage Cheese Filling Ingredients

- 2 cups / 500 ml dry curd cottage cheese
- 1 egg yolk, from the egg used in the dough
- 1 teaspoon / 5 ml salt
- ¼ teaspoon / 1 ml pepper

Cottage Cheese Filling Instructions

1. Mix together well.

Sauerkraut, Hamburger, and Potato Filling Ingredients

- ½ pound / 250 g lean ground beef
- ½ teaspoon / 2 ml pepper
- ½ teaspoon / 2 ml salt
- 1 large potato, boiled, mashed and cooled
- 1 cup / 250 ml sauerkraut, well drained

Sauerkraut, Hamburger, and Potato Filling Instructions

1. Fry ground beef, season, and add mashed potatoes and sauerkraut.
2. Cool.

Fruit Filling Ingredients

- Fresh plums, cut in half
- Fresh raspberries
- Sugar

Fruit Filling Instructions

1. Place half a plum or several raspberries every few inches along the rolled out *Wareneki* dough. Add a pinch of sugar over raspberries before closing.

Cooking Instructions

1. Bring to boil lightly salted water in a large saucepan.
2. Drop fresh or frozen *Wareneki* into boiling water and boil for 5 minutes if fresh or 10 minutes if frozen. *Wareneki* will float when they are cooked.
3. Drain immediately.
4. Serve with gravy (recipe follows).

Wareneki Gravy Ingredients

- ¼ cup / 60 ml butter
- 1 cup / 250 ml sour cream or whipping cream
- Salt and pepper

Wareneki Gravy Instructions

1. In a small saucepan, melt butter; stir in cream.
2. Bring to a light boil; reduce heat to simmer.
3. Salt and pepper to taste if using sour cream.
4. Simmer 5–10 minutes.

TIP: When cottage cheese *Wareneki* are boiled and drained, fry them in butter along with onions and/or bacon. In a skillet, melt several spoons of butter (or bacon drippings) and add thinly sliced onions. When the onions begin to caramelize, add the boiled *Wareneki* and sauté until they turn crispy and golden. Serve with gravy or sour cream and crumbled bacon.

When serving *Wareneki* with fruit filling, use whipping cream instead of sour cream in gravy and omit salt and pepper. Sprinkle with sugar.

—*Kathy*

Wareneki is a very well known Russian Mennonite dish, often served with farmer sausage or ham, along with sautéed red cabbage (recipe on page 89), caramelized onions, and vegetables. Cottage cheese is the filling that I grew up with, but now I also make the meat and potato filling, which is more Ukrainian. The sour cream gravy adds a wonderful flavor to these plump little boiled pockets; if you choose to fry them, they are even more flavorful.

For a great finale to the meal serve plum and raspberry *Wareneki* with fresh cream and a sprinkle of sugar.

Kathy says

Wareneki (Cottage Cheese Pockets)

Serves 6

- ½ cup / 125 ml cream-style cottage cheese
- 1 large egg
- ¼ cup plus 1 tablespoon / 75 ml milk
- 1 teaspoon / 5 ml oil
- ½ cup / 70 g white corn flour
- ¼ cup / 30 g white bean flour
- ¼ cup / 40 g potato starch
- ¼ cup / 30 g tapioca starch
- 2 teaspoons / 14 g xanthan gum
- ½ teaspoon / 5 g salt

TIP: Because the success of gluten-free baking depends on consistent and accurate measurements, the weight (grams) conversions for dry ingredients are included in all gluten-free recipes.

1. In a blender, mix first 4 ingredients until smooth.
2. Measure dry ingredients into a zip-close plastic bag; mix thoroughly.
3. Pour liquid ingredients into mixer bowl and add the dry ingredients. Mix well.
4. Remove dough to a surface dusted with sweet rice flour; knead lightly until smooth. Use as little flour as necessary, keeping dough soft.
5. Roll out dough as thinly as possible.
6. Make Kathy's cottage cheese filling (recipe on page 90).
7. Drop teaspoons of filling an inch apart and in from edge of dough; fold dough over filling. Use a round cookie cutter or a glass to cut individual *Wareneki*.
8. Moisten fingers with a bit of oil and firmly pinch together the edges of *Wareneki*.
9. Serve with cream gravy, fried onions, and farmer sausage.

TIP: Freeze *Wareneki* before cooking to ensure a lasting seal on edges. Drop frozen *Wareneki* into boiling water to which 1 tablespoon / 15 ml oil has been added. When water returns to a full boil, reduce heat and continue to boil for 5 minutes. Drain and then pan fry in butter until lightly browned.

Cream Gravy
- ½ onion, chopped
- ¼ cup / 50 g butter
- 1 tablespoon / 7 g cornstarch
- 1 teaspoon / 8 g sweet rice flour
- 1½ cup / 400 ml milk or cream

1. Fry onion in butter until lightly browned.
2. Mix cornstarch with rice flour.
3. Stir into milk or cream.
4. Add to onions and butter; cook, stirring until thickened.

TIP: This dough for *Wareneki* handles easily and the *Wareneki* taste every bit as good as the wheat ones. I doubt anyone could tell the difference!

No one ever told our Mennonite grandmothers, who really knew how to cook, that the phrase, "*Ach, das schmeckt aber gut!*" (Oh, but that tastes good!) really means "Oh my, what a lot of calories!"

Julie says

Kielke (Noodles) **Variation**

Serves 6

1. Follow the recipe for gluten-free *Wareneki*. Roll dough out as thinly as possible, using sweet rice flour for dusting your counter and dough.
2. Dust top of dough. Roll up the dough, beginning at one end; the fatter the roll the longer your noodles will be.
3. Cut off the roll from the rest of the dough and repeat, making another roll and cutting off until dough is used up.
4. Then slice roll into very narrow slices and unroll them. Allow the pile of noodles to dry on the counter.
5. Drop them into boiling water and boil until tender.
6. Strain, then pan fry in butter or oil until lightly browned. They brown quickly.
7. Serve with cream gravy and fried onions.

—*Julie*

Roast Turkey with Stuffing

Serves 10–12

- 1 12–15 pound / 5–7 kg turkey
- ¼ cup / 60 ml butter, cut into ½ inch / 1.25 cm pieces
- Olive or vegetable oil
- Salt
- Turkey stuffing (recipe follows)

1. Preheat oven to 325° F / 160° C.
2. Remove giblet package and neck from turkey cavity.
3. Wash turkey thoroughly and pat dry the cavity and the outside of the bird.
4. Carefully push your fingers under the skin of the turkey breast, creating a pocket on each side of the breastbone.
5. Push a piece of butter into each pocket; this will baste the turkey while it roasts.
6. Generously salt the turkey cavity. Place stuffing into cavity by handfuls until cavity is loosely packed.
7. Tuck drumstick ends into the ring of skin and skewer shut if necessary.
8. Fill neck end with stuffing and skewer the skin flap over it.
9. Place remaining stuffing onto a large piece of foil and package it, leaving a small opening. Set aside.
10. Generously rub outside of the turkey with oil and salt.
11. Place in a roasting pan, breast side up, and roast according to table below. Loosely tent the bird with foil if it begins to brown too much.
12. About 1 hour before turkey is done, add the stuffing package to the roasting pan to bake. The turkey is done when the drumstick moves easily when twisted. The juices should run clear when the meat is pierced and a meat thermometer registers 180° F / 82° C when inserted into the thickest part of the thigh.
13. Remove pan from the oven and let stand, tented with foil, 15–20 minutes before carving.
14. Transfer turkey to carving board and pour drippings in a saucepan for the gravy.
15. Remove stuffing from turkey and put in a serving bowl; mix lightly with stuffing from package. Keep warm until ready to serve.
16. Carve turkey and place on serving platter.
17. Make gravy (recipe follows).

TIP: When preparing any poultry, always have a sink of hot soapy water ready so that you can wash your hands and utensils frequently. Salmonella poisoning can occur if you do not thoroughly wash your hands and any surfaces the poultry has touched.

If turkey is frozen, leave in its original packaging and thaw in the refrigerator, allowing 5 hours per pound.

ROASTING CHART

(oven temperature: 325° F / 160° C)

Pounds / kg	Hours (for stuffed turkey)
8–10 / 3.5–4.5	3¼–3½
10–12 / 4.5–5.5	3–3¼
12–16 / 5.5–7.0	3¼–4
16–22 / 7.0–10.0	4–4½

Turkey Stuffing

- 12–14 cups / 3 L cubed day old bread
- ½ cup / 125 ml butter
- 2 cups / 500 ml chopped onion
- 2 cups / 500 ml chopped celery, including the leaves
- Salt and pepper to taste
- 1 tablespoon / 15 ml poultry seasoning
- 1–1½ cup / 250–375 ml raisins
- 1 cup / 250 ml dried cranberries or prunes, cut up (or cut up apples or dried apricots)

1. Place bread cubes in large bowl with raisins and cranberries.
2. Sauté onions and celery in butter over medium heat until soft and translucent.
3. Pour sautéed mixture over bread mixture; add poultry seasoning, salt, and pepper.
4. Mix lightly until ingredients are evenly distributed. Stuff the turkey as directed above.

Turkey Gravy

- Liquid from turkey drippings
- 1 cup / 250 ml hot water
- ¼ cup / 60 ml flour
- 1 cup / 250 ml cold water

1. After removing turkey from roasting pan to carving board, pour turkey drippings into a saucepan.
2. Add hot water to the roasting pan. Scrape up the brown bits in the pan, adding them to the drippings in the saucepan. Bring saucepan contents to a boil.
3. In a shaker or glass jar, blend flour and cold water until smooth.
4. Whisk flour/water mixture into turkey drippings, stirring constantly. Add salt and pepper to taste.
5. Continue to boil until thickened to desired consistency, adding more flour/ water as necessary.

—Bev

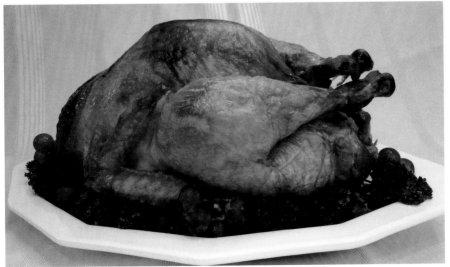

Roasted Chicken with Anise Seeds and *Bubbat* (Bread)

Serves 6

- **1 large fryer or roasting chicken, cut up into pieces with the bone and skin**
- **Salt**

- **2 tablespoons / 30 ml anise seed**
- **1 tablespoon / 15 ml flour**
- **1 cup / 250 ml milk**

1. Arrange the chicken pieces in a single layer in a dark enameled roasting pan with a lid.
2. Sprinkle with salt and anise seed.
3. Cover and bake at 325° F / 160° C for 2½ hours.
4. Remove from the oven. Take out ½ cup of the drippings if making *Bubbat*.
5. Increase oven heat to 350° F / 175° C. Add ½ cup water to the roasting pan and return to the oven, uncovered.
6. Prepare the *Bubbat* and bake alongside the chicken for another 30 minutes.
7. Remove the chicken to a serving plate and cover with foil to stay warm.
8. Sprinkle flour into the pan with the drippings. Cook and stir over medium heat until bubbly.
9. Add milk, stirring until bubbly. Add more milk, according to desired gravy consistency
10. Serve with new boiled or mashed potatoes.

TIP: While this chicken can be roasted in any roasting pan, I find it develops the nicest color in the speckled dark blue roasting pan that is inexpensive and widely available.

My mom-by-love Pauline taught me how to make this roasted chicken with its wonderful aroma. In their family it was nicknamed "sticky chicken" because the skin caramelizes with the slow roast, and, if you eat the drumstick with your hands, things get sticky.

She always serves *Bubbat* on the side. *Bubbat* is a little like cornbread without the cornmeal.

Lovella says

Bubbat

- 2 cups / 500 ml flour
- 1 tablespoon / 15 ml baking powder
- 1 teaspoon / 5 ml salt
- ¼ cup / 60 ml sugar
- 1 cup / 250 ml milk
- 2 eggs
- ½ cup / 125 ml chicken drippings
- 1½ cup / 350 ml raisins

1. Combine the dry ingredients in a medium sized mixing bowl.
2. Combine the milk, eggs, and chicken drippings. Add to the dry ingredients.
3. Add the raisins and stir until combined.
4. Pour the batter into an 8 x 8-inch / 20 x 20-cm pan greased with no-stick cooking spray.
5. Bake alongside the chicken for 30 minutes.

TIP: Omit the raisins or add other dried fruits to the *Bubbat*. Another option is to use *Bubbat* to stuff a roasting chicken. If you bake the *Bubbat* in the chicken, omit the chicken drippings, using butter instead. The *Bubbat* is naturally moist with the chicken drippings baked right into the *Bubbat*.

—*Lovella*

Who's Cooking

Bev's Story

Family and faith have had the most influence in my life. I grew up in Ontario with my mom's family close by. One of my early memories is of sitting on a big bed with my cousins listening to my grandmother tell stories from her youth in Russia, and also stories from the Bible.

My Dad's family lived in British Columbia, so a trip across the country every few years became part of the family budget. A friendship built while visiting family in British Columbia ultimately led to meeting my husband.

Harv and I have only one sibling each. Over the years, our families have melded into one. When my parents came west to join us for Christmas or Thanksgiving, both families would gather at our home, with all the women working together in the kitchen. We had so much fun as we cooked, served, and washed dishes.

Both my mother and mother-in-law taught me how to prepare many traditional Mennonite recipes. In canning season, four generations worked together. The children pulled grapes off the stem for fruit cocktail, while Great-Grandma peeled peaches and pears, and Mom and I sterilized and filled jars. Every fall, we spent a whole day making apple juice, with the children washing the apples, the men grinding and pressing the apples, and the women heating the juice and filling the jars.

I've always enjoyed baking and cooking. My mother worked out of the home, so my sister and I were expected to help with the Saturday chores. My job was to do the baking for the week, which included a cake, several types of squares, cookies, and perhaps a pie. All this food was required for either Sunday guests or weekday lunches.

Mom entertained a lot. She taught me how setting a beautiful table can make your guests feel special. Even for family suppers, she insisted on a clean tablecloth and proper serving dishes. Food was never brought to the table in a

cooking pot. She was not afraid of trying new recipes, so there was always a wide variety of food in our home.

When I was in junior high, I started my own recipe collection, painstakingly writing out recipes and cutting pictures out of magazines. Today I enjoy entertaining and love trying new recipes. This love of cooking has filtered down the generations so that now even our young grandchildren want to help.

The faith lived out by my grandparents and parents set an example of putting God first in my life. I learned from them how important it is to give freely of my time and resources and to take an active part in my local church.

But from everlasting to everlasting the Lord's love is with those who fear him, and his righteousness with their children's children. —PSALM 103:17 (*NIV*)

Chicken Enchiladas

Serves 6

- **8 large flour tortillas**
- **1 cup / 250 ml green salsa**
- **½ cup / 125 ml guacamole**
- **1 cup / 250 ml cheddar cheese, grated**
- **¼ cup / 60 ml green onions, sliced**
- **1 cup / 250 ml chopped tomatoes**
- **4 cups / 1000 ml chicken, cooked and shredded**
- **Sliced peppers as garnish (optional)**

1. Use a whole roasted chicken (purchased from the deli or cooked at home). Remove the skin and bones and shred the meat.
2. Combine salsa, guacamole, cheese, onions, and tomatoes. Stir in shredded chicken.
3. Lay tortillas on a flat surface and place equal amounts of the chicken mixture on top.
4. Roll up tortillas and place in a greased 9 x 13-inch / 22 x 33-cm glass baking pan.
5. Make enchilada sauce and cheese sauce (recipes follow) and pour over the tortillas.
6. Sprinkle generously with extra grated cheese.
7. Bake in 350° F / 175° C oven for 30–40 minutes.
8. Garnish with sliced peppers and additional green onions if desired.
9. Serve with sour cream, guacamole, and tortilla chips.

Enchilada sauce

1. Make 1 envelope of purchased enchilada sauce according to package directions.
2. Pour over wrapped tortillas.

In our home we like spicy food so I use hot salsa. When I make this dish for company, I usually choose mild salsa and put out a jar of hot salsa for those who prefer added heat.

Kathy says

Cheese sauce

- **½ cup / 125 ml Velveeta or other processed cheese loaf**
- **1 cup / 250 ml cup canned diced tomatoes**
- **½ cup / 125 ml chunky salsa**
- **Cheddar and mozzarella cheese, grated**

1. Place first 3 ingredients in a bowl and microwave until cheese is melted.
2. Stir to mix and pour cheese sauce over enchiladas.
3. Add extra cheese as desired.

TIP: Serve with Spanish rice and a salad of shredded lettuce and tomatoes.

—Kathy

Quesadillas / Tortilla Shells

Yields 12

Tortilla shells

- 1⅓ cup / 300 ml milk
- 1 tablespoon / 15 ml olive oil
- 1¾ cups / 180 g tapioca starch
- ¾ cups / 105 g white corn flour
- ¼ cup / 35 g white bean flour
- 2 teaspoons / 15 g xanthan gum
- ½ teaspoon / 5 g salt
- ½ teaspoon / 5 g baking powder

1. Pour milk and oil in mixer bowl.
2. Blend dry ingredients well and add all at once to liquids.
3. Mix on low speed until blended, then beat on high for 2 minutes.
4. Turn dough onto a surface dusted with sweet rice flour.
5. Knead until smooth. Completely cover dough in plastic wrap. Let rest for 30 minutes.
6. Divide into 12 pieces. Place these pieces on a plate and cover with a damp towel.
7. Roll each piece into a thin circle using a 9-inch / 22-cm plate as a template. Cut off excess and add to next piece. It is easier to begin with 2 pieces of dough to roll out the first circle. You should be left with enough excess at the end to make the 12th circle.
8. To transfer dough circles to a plate, fold each one in half, then in half again, then unfold on the plate. Stack circles, separating each with plastic wrap or wax paper.
9. Heat a skillet with a small amount of oil; fry each tortilla for 30 seconds on each side until very lightly browned.
10. Stack, cool, and store in zip-close plastic bags in fridge. They will keep for several days.

TIP: Do not use cornmeal as a substitute for corn flour. However, you can use white cornmeal if it is very finely ground.

Having my daughter and family over for dinner can be a cooking challenge. Of the six of us, three have celiac. Considering other food preferences and allergies, I rarely can plan one menu. But when I make these quesadillas, everyone is happy, including me!

Julie says

Quesadillas

- Gluten-free tortillas
- Cheese, grated
- Onions, fried
- Green peppers, chopped
- Cooked chicken or beef, sliced

1. On one half of each tortilla, layer grated cheese, fried onions, and green peppers, cooked slices of chicken or beef, ending with more cheese. Fold the other half of the tortilla over the mixture.
2. Fry in skillet on both sides until golden brown and cheese is melted.
3. Serve hot with salsa and sour cream.

TIP: If cooking for a crowd, make these ahead. Keep them warm in the oven.

—Julie

Chicken Quesadillas with Caramelized Onions and Peppers

Serves 4–8

Growing up in the Los Angeles area of California, my family grew to enjoy and appreciate Mexican dishes. Our Hispanic neighbors shared their cooking heritage with us. Since moving to Washington State, I've incorporated many favorite Mexican dishes in my weekly meals. They are simple to make and very economical.

Ellen says

- 2 cups / 500 ml cooked chicken, cubed or shredded
- 1 large onion, thinly sliced
- 2 bell peppers, thinly sliced (1 green and 1 yellow, orange, or red)
- 2 tablespoons / 30 ml olive oil
- 2 cups / 500 ml medium cheddar cheese, grated
- 8 - 10-inch / 25-cm flour tortillas
- Cilantro (optional)

1. Heat oil in a 10-inch / 25-cm non-stick skillet; add onion and peppers until onions are caramelized. Remove and set aside.
2. Sprinkle a small amount of grated cheese in the hot pan. Place 1 tortilla on top of the cheese and pat it down on the cheese. Layer the chicken, onions and peppers, cilantro and more cheese. Place another tortilla on top of the filling.
3. When the cheese has melted slightly and the tortilla can be easily lifted from the skillet, carefully flip the quesadilla and heat thoroughly.
4. Slide the quesadilla from the skillet to a cutting board. Repeat the process to make 4 quesadillas.
5. Cut each quesadilla into 6 pieces.
6. Serve with your choice of guacamole, sour cream, salsa, and salad.

TIP: Putting the cheese in first doesn't make it burn. Rather, the cheese ends up adhering to the tortilla as opposed to the pan. This also crisps up the tortilla slightly so you have a different result than a soft quesadilla. You should use a non-stick skillet for this method.

—Ellen

A BRIDGE PROVIDED

The land which you cross over to possess is a land of hills and valleys, which drinks water from the rain of heaven. —DEUTERONOMY 11:11 (*NKJV*)

God called his ancient people to possess a land that was good and desires the same for his children today. What we sometimes don't realize is that in order to get to the good land, God's people had to do a seemingly impossible task, cross a rushing river. But God provided a way for them to cross it safely.

Every one of us faces crises in life where we must confront unforeseen, devastating situations such as a financial loss, death of a loved one, wrongful treatment, broken friendships, a tragedy or health crisis, or personal disappointment.

Whatever our crisis, we fear what lies before us and we become anxious, not knowing where to turn or how to cross the difficulty that lies in our life path. In fact, crossing over seems impossible. But God's promises are true.

> *When you pass through the waters, I will be with you; And through the rivers, they shall not overflow you. When you walk through the fire, you shall not be burned, Nor shall the flame scorch you.* —ISAIAH 43:2 (*NKJV*)

No matter what lies before us, we can trust that God will build a bridge for us. He will make a way for us to cross over. No matter how frightening and huge our situation looms, with childlike faith we can walk safely over the rushing river to the good land that awaits us on the other side.

—Julie

Anneliese says

Barbecued Salmon with Sun-Dried Tomatoes

Serves 6

- 1 (2½ pounds / 1 kg) salmon fillet
- 5 garlic cloves, finely chopped
- ¼ cup / 60 ml fresh parsley, finely chopped
- 2 tablespoons / 30 ml fresh basil, finely chopped
- ⅓ cup / 75 ml sun-dried tomatoes in oil, drained and chopped
- ¾ teaspoon / 3 ml salt
- ¼ cup / 60 ml olive oil

1. For topping, combine all ingredients except the salmon in a jar and refrigerate a few hours or overnight.
2. Place salmon on greased or parchment paper-lined foil pan. Set over low heat on the barbecue. Close top and cook 10 minutes.
3. Spread topping over fillet.
4. Close top, raise temperature to medium and cook another 15–25 minutes. Fish is done when it flakes easily with a fork.

—Anneliese

Coconut Prawns

Yields approximately 35 prawns

- 2 pounds / 1 kg large, raw prawns, deveined
- 1 cup / 250 ml flour
- ½ teaspoon / 2 ml seasoned salt
- ¼ teaspoon / 1 ml ground pepper
- ½ teaspoon / 2 ml ginger (optional) or red pepper flakes for more spice
- 3 egg whites
- 2 cups / 500 ml coconut, flaked
- Oil

1. Remove shells from prawns, leaving tail shells intact.
2. Mix seasonings with flour in shallow bowl.
3. Beat egg whites just until they are foamy and soft peaks form. Do not over-beat or the egg white will not stick to the prawns.
4. Place coconut in another shallow bowl.
5. Coat each prawn with seasoned flour; dip in egg white until well coated; and coat gently on all sides with coconut.
6. Fry in 1-inch / 2.54-cm oil over medium heat, turning once. Cook until the coconut is golden brown and the prawns have turned pink. To check, cut one prawn in half.
7. Drain on paper towel and serve.

TIP: The largest prawns or shrimp work best. Using raw ones ensures that they do not overcook and become rubbery.

—Bev

We first tasted coconut prawns about eight years ago on the Island of Roataán, Honduras, where our oldest son was working as a missionary. The prawns were truly memorable and I asked him to get a recipe for me. The first time I made them was in our camper on a trip to the Maritimes. Each town on the Gaspé Peninsula had its own fresh fish shop and we treated ourselves to fresh shrimp and lobster at every opportunity. If you make these once, I guarantee you'll make them again.

Bev says

Basil Tomato Pizza

Pizza crust
- 3–3½ cups / 750–900 ml flour
- 1 teaspoon / 5 ml sugar
- 1 teaspoon / 5 ml salt
- 1 tablespoon / 15 ml instant yeast
- 2 tablespoons / 30 ml oil
- 1¼ cup / 310 ml warm water
- 1–2 tablespoons cornmeal

Basil Tomato Topping
- ½ cup / 125 ml mayonnaise
- ½ cup / 125 ml Parmesan cheese, grated
- 1 large garlic clove, minced
- 1 teaspoon / 5 ml dried basil leaves or ⅓ cup / 75 ml fresh basil, chopped
- 3–4 seeded Roma tomatoes, thinly sliced
- 1–1½ cup / 250–375 ml mozzarella cheese, coarsely grated
- 1 teaspoon / 5 ml fresh chives or green onions, chopped fine

Served as a meal or as an appetizer, this is a nice change from a tomato sauce-based pizza.

Bev says

1. Mix 3 cups / 750 ml flour with the sugar, salt, and yeast in a mixing bowl.
2. Add oil and warm water and mix. Continue adding flour to make a soft dough that is no longer sticky.
3. Cover and let rise until nearly double in bulk.
4. Grease a large pizza pan or cookie sheet and sprinkle with cornmeal. This will keep the crust from getting soggy.
5. Roll out dough on a floured surface and place on prepared pan, or just press it out, stretching it to fit the pan.
6. For topping, combine mayonnaise, Parmesan cheese, garlic, and basil until well mixed. Spread on prepared crust.
7. Arrange tomato slices over topping and sprinkle with chives and grated cheese.
8. Bake at 425° F / 220° C for 15 minutes or until bubbling and beginning to brown.

TIP: If you don't have time to make the homemade crust, substitute a prepared crust available in the deli section of the grocery store.

Also, this recipe can be used to make two medium-sized pizza crusts rather than one large. Freeze one for another day.

—Bev

Pizza Crust

- ½ cup / 75 ml warm water
- 1 teaspoon / 7 g sugar
- 1 teaspoon / 6 g gelatin
- 1 rounded tablespoon / 10 g active dry yeast
- 1 teaspoon / 5 ml olive oil
- ¼ cup / 60 ml milk
- ½ cup / 70 g white bean flour
- ¼ cup / 40 g millet flour
- ½ cup / 80 g potato starch
- ¼ cup / 30 g tapioca starch
- 1 teaspoon / 10 g xanthan gum
- ½ teaspoon / 5 g salt
- Sweet rice flour for rolling
- Cornmeal for dusting pan

1. Mix 1 teaspoon sugar and 1 teaspoon gelatin in a cup. Whisk in the warm water and then the yeast. Set the cup in warm water to keep yeast warm. Let proof until doubled.
2. Pour oil and milk into mixer bowl; add proofed yeast. Mix lightly.
3. Blend dry ingredients well, then add all at once to the liquid mixture.
4. Mix on low until blended, then beat on high for 3 minutes.
5. Turn out on a surface sprinkled with sweet rice flour; knead lightly.
6. Roll out to form a 13-inch / 33-cm circle. Then roll the edge under to form a thicker edge.
7. Cut parchment paper to fit pizza pan and dust with cornmeal.
8. Carefully transfer pizza crust onto parchment paper.
9. Bake at 400° F / 205° C for 20 minutes.
10. Remove from oven, cool slightly, then spread with pizza sauce and your favorite toppings.
11. Return to oven and bake another 20 minutes or until pizza is done. If crust edges brown too quickly cover them with strips of foil.

—Julie

I love this pizza crust. Roll it thin, leave it thicker, or make it however you like it.

Julie says

On Easter Sunday, our traditional Mennonite meal included baked ham, *Plumamoos*, *Zwieback*, either scalloped potatoes or potato salad and Paska, of course. I remember the long tables set up in my Grandma's basement, loaded with wonderful foods, and lined from one end to the other with much loved uncles, aunts, and cousins.

There was a lot of happy noise as adults visited and we children ran up and down the stairs, excited to be with our cousins. I remember eating the raisin sauce with ham in those days. Now, if there is *Plumamoos* on the menu, I prefer to serve the mustard sauce. I first tasted this sauce at our church, where it always accompanied a ham dinner. It is sweet and creamy with just a bit of bite, and complements the ham to perfection. It is now the favorite condiment for baked ham at our house.

Bev says

Baked Ham with Sauces

Serves 10, depending on size of ham

- **1 fully cooked bone-in ham, whole or half**
- **1 cup / 250 ml water**

1. Place cut side down (if doing a half) in roasting pan. Add water, covering tightly with foil.
2. Bake according to package directions. A good rule of thumb for baking time is 17–20 minutes per pound to an internal temperature of 160° F / 70 ° C. Place the thermometer in the thickest part of the ham, not too near a bone.
3. To serve, slice the ham and serve hot or cold with a sauce.
4. There are several ways to slice a whole or half ham:
   - Slice a thin piece off the bottom of the ham so it sits securely on the cutting board. Starting at the shank end, and using a sharp knife, cut parallel slices into the meat. Then cut across the bottom of the cuts to remove slices. Turn the ham over and repeat the process.
   - If you carve the ham in the kitchen rather than at the table cut a large piece from the bone, keeping in mind the shape of the slice you want. Then slice each piece into even slices.
5. Save the bone for Anneliese's green bean soup recipe (page 50).

Mustard Sauce

- ⅔ cup / 150 ml sugar
- 1 tablespoon / 15 ml dry mustard
- 4 eggs
- ¼ cup / 60 ml vinegar
- 1 tablespoon / 15 ml butter

1. Mix dry ingredients first.
2. Beat eggs until lemon-colored and fluffy.
3. Gradually add dry ingredients and vinegar.
4. Microwave on high for 1 minute, or cook over medium heat, stirring constantly until mixture thickens.
5. Stir well. Continue to microwave at 1 minute intervals using a lower power, stirring each time until mixture thickens but is still creamy. You will need to watch carefully that it does not overcook or it will lose its creamy texture. Do not allow it to bubble.
6. Stir in butter and cool.
7. Refrigerate until serving. Serve either hot or cold with baked ham.
8. Store any leftovers in the fridge.

TIP: This is also delicious spread on ham or sausage sandwiches.

Raisin Sauce

- ¼ cup / 60 ml brown sugar
- 3 tablespoons / 45 ml cornstarch
- 1½ cup / 375 ml water
- ¼ cup / 60 ml vinegar
- ½ cup / 125 ml sultana raisins, washed
- Juice and rind of ½ lemon or orange

1. Blend dry ingredients in glass bowl or saucepan.
2. Add liquids and stir well.
3. Stir in raisins, juice, and rind.
4. Microwave at 1 minute intervals, stirring each time, or cook over medium heat on stove.
5. Cook until sauce thickens and begins to bubble.
6. Serve warm with baked ham or roast pork.

TIP: Use some of the broth from the ham as part of the water, but keep in mind that it will taste saltier.

—Bev

Who's Cooking

Julie's Story

My living generations stretch from my mother to my granddaughters. I loved watching my daughter, Romay, and now my two granddaughters, Elise and Elora, grow up. I have observed their natural interests and gifts. As I look back over the years to my own childhood, I remember four insightful moments that determined my life path.

The first came when I was about four years old. I was sitting in my grandmother's kitchen when I leaned over to see the pictures in the book my aunt was reading. There were none. I was excited when she told me that the funny black marks all over the pages were words: I couldn't wait to learn to read.

How I love books! Each new book in my hands stirs in me a great feeling of anticipation. Books feed my love of learning, and what I learn I love to share, whether it is in a teaching situation, in private conversation, or in my writing. Now I am learning how to cook and bake gluten-free foods, since my daughter, granddaughter, and I have celiac, an auto-immune genetic disorder involving the intolerance of gluten.

Another defining moment came when I was around ten years old. I was riding my bike, house to house in my rural neighborhood, selling raffle tickets for my school. One elderly couple invited me in. In the few minutes I spent in their home, the love they showed each other made a lasting impression on me. I noted the gentle way they spoke to each other, the tenderness in their glances, the way they read each other's thoughts. They became the model for the kind of marriage I wanted. I married young, just after my 18th birthday, and after 45 years of marriage, my husband and I still love each other!

A career-determining moment came one day when we were visiting my aunt and uncle. Admiring a lacy crocheted swan sitting on the dining room floor, I was amazed that my aunt had hand-crafted it. I decided that one day I, too, would make beautiful things with my hands. Since then, a sewing machine has been an important part of my life. I have been a dressmaker and an alterations specialist. I have operated a drapery/decorating business, and have done a few other things in between. Being self-employed for most of my working years has allowed me great freedom to fit all the things that are important to me into my life, including being home for my daughter, and later being available for my precious granddaughters.

The greatest moment that determined my life path came when I was eight years old. As I listened to a German storybook being read to me, I became convicted of my need for God's forgiveness. When I asked Jesus into my heart, I was filled with joy and decided I wanted to be a missionary in Africa. I never went to Africa, but my love for God and my desire to know him is at the core of my being. Of all the books in the world my very favorite is the Bible and I never tire of its truth and beauty.

Green Bean Stew

Serves 6

- 1½ pound / 750 g ring farmer sausage, cut into 2-inch / 5-cm pieces and sliced in half
- 4 large potatoes, peeled and diced
- 6 carrots, sliced
- 2 pounds / 1 kilogram green beans, cut into 1-inch / 2.5-cm pieces
- 2 large onions, diced
- 1 tablespoon / 15 ml summer savory
- ½ cup fresh parsley, chopped
- 1 teaspoon / 5 ml salt
- ½ teaspoon / 2 ml pepper
- 2 cups / 500 ml hot water

1. Place the sausage in the bottom of a heavy pot or in a large crock pot.
2. Layer the vegetables over the sausage in the order listed.
3. Sprinkle the seasonings on top.
4. Add hot water and cover.
5. Bake in the oven at 350° F / 175° C for 3 hours or in the crock pot on low for 6–8 hours.

—Lovella

My mother-in-law Pauline taught me how to make this recipe. I would phone her every year when the green beans were ripe on the bean pole and ask her what all went into this recipe. This stew has a fantastic fragrance. It might not be the prettiest stew, as the beans lose their bright green color, but the flavor is great; if there are any leftovers, they are eaten quickly the next day.

Lovella says

Mennonites have used dried fruit liberally in recipes such as stuffing (*Bubbat*), stewed cabbage, and *Obstsuppe* (*Plumimoos*). Having grown up with this flavor, I was quick to try this modern-day recipe, which has become a favorite. I like to serve this recipe with stewed red cabbage.

Anneliese says

Stuffed Pork Loin

Serves 6

- 3 pound / 1½ kg pork loin or rib roast
- 2 tablespoons / 30 ml butter
- 2 apples, cut into ½-inch / 1.5-cm pieces
- ⅓ cup / 75 ml dried apricots, chopped
- ⅓ cup / 75 ml prunes, chopped
- 3 tablespoons / 45 ml frozen orange juice concentrate
- 1–2 tablespoons / 15–30 ml fresh thyme, minced
- Salt and pepper to taste
- ½ teaspoon / 2 ml cinnamon

1. In a small saucepan, melt butter; add apples and cook about 5 minutes, stirring until lightly browned.
2. Add apricots, prunes, and juice, and continue cooking until fruit is tender and liquid has evaporated.
3. Season with half the thyme, salt, and pepper. Cool.
4. Cut a pocket into side of roast. Fill it with this mixture. Tie the roast shut with kitchen twine.
5. Season roast with remaining thyme, salt, pepper, and add the cinnamon.
6. Spray the roasting pan with oil and bake uncovered at 350° F / 175° C for 30 minutes.
7. Cover and bake another 60–75 minutes, until meat thermometer inserted in center shows 160° F / 71° C.
8. Remove from oven onto plate, tent loosely with foil and let sit for 15 minutes before serving.

TIP: Add cut up potatoes, yams, carrots and left over fruit filling to the roasting pan for the final hour. When the roast is resting, remove the vegetables onto a serving platter. Mix a tablespoon of flour with 1 cup of water and add it to the drippings in the pot, stirring to make a gravy to drizzle over the roast. Season to taste.

—Anneliese

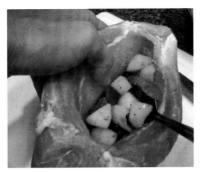
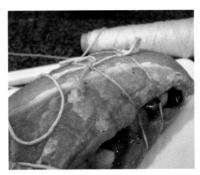

Breads

These buns have been a family favorite for more years, than I care to count! My mom-in-law made excellent *Zwieback*, and since I couldn't compete with Grandma's *Zwieback*, I made these refrigerator rolls as my trademark recipe. Now I'm a grandma and though I bake *Zwieback* as well, it's these melt-in-your-mouth rolls that the grands request.

I always make a double batch, often making cinnamon buns with a portion of the dough. It's the perfect recipe for those times when you are expecting overnight guests. You can have freshly baked buns for breakfast with little or no fuss. How handy or efficient is that?

Judy says

Refrigerator Potato Rolls

Yields 32 buns

- **2 cups / 500 ml very warm water**
- **¼ cup / 60 ml instant mashed potato flakes**
- **½ cup / 125 ml sugar**
- **1 tablespoon / 15 ml salt**
- **2 eggs, beaten**
- **½ cup / 125 ml butter or margarine, softened**
- **2 tablespoons / 30 ml instant yeast**
- **6½ cups / 1500 ml flour**

1. Stir together the water, potato flakes, sugar, and salt.
2. Add eggs and butter, then yeast mixed with 3 cups / 750 ml flour. Beat with mixer on high speed.
3. Add remaining flour, ½ cup / 125 ml at a time, until the dough can be easily handled. Knead well.
4. Place in a greased, covered bowl in the refrigerator to rest for at least 2 hours or overnight.
5. Divide dough into 4 equal portions; roll each piece into a circle on a buttered surface.
6. Cut each circle into 8 wedges; roll each wedge to form a crescent shape.
7. Let rise until doubled in size, at least 1 hour.
8. Bake at 375° F / 190° C for 12–15 minutes.

TIP: You can also use this dough to make cinnamon buns.

—Judy

Zwieback (Double-decker Rolls)

Yields 4 dozen

- 1½ tablespoons / 22 ml active dry yeast
- 1 teaspoon / 5 ml sugar
- 1 cup / 250 ml warm water
- 3 cups / 750 ml warm milk
- ¼ cup / 60 ml instant mashed potato flakes
- 3 tablespoons / 45 ml oil
- 2 teaspoons /10 ml salt
- 1 cup / 250 ml soft butter (no substitutes)
- 7½–7¾ cups / 1.7–1.8 L all purpose flour, plus a little more for dusting

1. Add yeast and sugar to warm water in a small bowl. Let rest for 10 minutes.
2. Heat milk until it is just warm or at room temperature.
3. Add the potato flakes to the warm milk; stir, then blend in oil and salt.
4. In a large bowl, cut the butter into 3 cups / 750 ml flour using a pastry blender.
5. Stir the yeast and milk mixture into the flour and butter mixture.
6. Add another 4½ cups / 1 L of flour; turn the dough out onto a floured surface and knead until smooth. Add sprinkles of flour as needed to make a soft dough. Place the dough into a large mixing bowl. Cover and let rise until double in bulk, about 1 hour.
7. Grease 3 large cookie sheets or line them with parchment paper.
8. Take a piece of dough the size of an orange and hold it in your left hand with a part of it between your thumb and forefinger. With your right hand, squeeze a bit of dough between your thumb and forefinger, about the size of a walnut; pinch your thumb and forefinger together to squeeze it off. With your right hand take the dough and place it on the pan. Again, squeeze the dough between your thumb and forefinger, this time a smaller piece to make the top bun. Squeeze it off and place it on top of your first bun. With both index fingers, press down through the top and bottom buns to seal them together. Repeat with all the dough.
9. Cover the buns with a clean tea towel and let rise until double in size, about 1 hour.
10. Bake in a preheated 400° F / 205° C oven for 20 minutes or until golden brown.

—Lovella

Zwieback are small white double buns typically served at our Sunday evening meals; the meals are commonly referred to as *Faspa*. They are most often eaten with fresh churned butter and homemade jams and cheese.

My beloved's maternal grandmother, Agatha, secured the love of her grandson by tucking a bag of fresh *Zwieback* in the car with him before his family headed home. For a grown man to remember her so fondly motivated me to duplicate her *Zwieback* recipe, so that he could remember her sweet ways. Agatha and co-author Judy's mother-in-law, Nellie, were sisters. When we became blog friends, we realized very quickly that many of our family recipes were similar.

When company left after *Faspa* on Sundays, the remaining *Tweiback* (Low German spelling) were set aside to make *Reistche* the next day. To do this, the *Tweiback* would be taken apart and set on a cookie sheet to toast slowly in the oven. These rusks (the Mennonite version) were made by the thousands when the first Mennonites emigrated from Russia. Since these buns have a very long shelf life, the women made enough for their families, storing them with their few belongings to be eaten over the several months it took to cross the ocean and settle into their new homes.

Our grandparents survived on little else but *Reistche Tweiback* in those difficult times. Our generation now enjoys them dunked in hot coffee, then dabbed with a touch of butter before popping them into our mouths.

Lovella says

Buns and *Platz* (Coffee Cake)

Serves 8

- ½ cup / 125 ml butter
- 2 cups / 500 ml milk
- 2 cups / 500 ml water
- 3 eggs
- ¼ cup / 60 ml sugar
- 1 tablespoon / 15 ml salt
- ¼ cup / 60 ml oil
- 10 cups / 2250 ml flour (approximately)
- 2 tablespoons / 30 ml instant yeast

1. Using the microwave or stove top, melt butter and heat milk together. Add water, cold or warm, to make the combined liquids quite warm, about 100° F / 40° C.
2. In a large mixing bowl, beat eggs, adding the sugar and salt; add oil and warm liquids.
3. Add 4–5 cups / 1000 ml flour and the yeast, mixing well.
4. Switching to dough-hook attachment, if using a mixer, add the remaining flour, 1 cup at a time. Knead until all the flour is mixed in well and the dough is smooth and not sticky when touched with floured hands.
5. Turn dough into a larger bowl to rise, giving it a few more punches and turns to make it smooth.
6. Cover with a tea towel and a large plastic bag. Let rise until double, about 1–1½ hours.
7. Gently punch down dough. With greased hands form the dough into a smooth ball. Pinch off sections for the following uses.

Plain Buns
Yields 15-18 buns

1. Use half of the dough. With slightly greased hands, shape into buns by pinching off a good handful of dough at a time and then squeezing or pinching off buns between thumb and forefinger.
2. Place on greased cookie sheet. Cover with tea towel and plastic; let rise 1 hour.
3. Bake at 400° F / 205° C for 20 minutes. Remove from pan and cool on wire rack.

Cinnamon Buns
Yields 12–15

- 2 tablespoons / 30 ml butter, melted
- 1 cup / 250 ml brown sugar
- 1–2 teaspoons / 5–10 ml cinnamon

1. With greased hands, pinch off a large piece of the dough and roll into a rectangle shape on a floured surface.
2. Spread with butter and brown sugar mixed with cinnamon.
3. Roll up jellyroll style and cut into 1¼-inch / 3-cm slices.
4. Place on greased or parchment paper lined pan. Cover and let rise for 1 hour.
5. Bake at 350° F / 175° C for 20 minutes or until golden.
6. Remove from pan onto wire rack. When cool, ice with the following icing.

Icing

- 1½ cup / 375 ml icing or confectioners sugar
- 1 tablespoon / 15 ml soft butter
- Milk

1. Mix sugar, butter, and enough milk to make a nice spreading or drizzling consistency.

TIP: Slice the buns before freezing them. This makes it easy to make sandwiches to pack a lunch.

Platz

- Cut up fruit, such as plums or apricots
- 5 tablespoons / 75 ml butter, room temperature
- ¾ cup / 175 ml flour
- ¾ cup / 175 ml sugar

1. Grease a round spring-form pan or a 9 x 13-inch / 22 x 33-cm pan, depending on amount of dough used. Using your hands, spread or pat the dough into the pan, about ½-inch / 1.25-cm thick. Let rest 20–30 minutes.
2. Spread dough with cut up fruit, and sprinkle with a few tablespoons additional sugar.
3. To make crumbs, mix butter into flour and sugar using a pastry blender. Sprinkle crumbs on fruit using your hands.
4. Cover loosely and let rise 30–60 minutes.
5. Bake at 375° F / 190° C for 30 minutes.
6. Remove from pan and let cool on wire rack.

TIPS:

- Some people prefer a flat *Platz*; others a high *Platz*. Choose the pan size to determine the thickness of the dough.
- There are many options for toppings: My mother often covered the dough with a beaten egg for moisture, before adding the crumb topping. I like cherry pie filling: pat out the dough, spread with cherry pie filling, and then top with the crumbs.
- To keep crumbs crunchy, don't store baked *Platz* in a sealed container. Rather, just cover loosely with a tea towel. If you freeze *Platz*, uncover to thaw.

—*Anneliese*

My growing up memories of Saturdays are of my Mom cooking a big pot of soup and baking a batch of fresh buns. Usually she would take part of the dough to make *Platz* or, as we call it, *Streuselkuchen*. My husband's side of the family calls it *Riebelplatz*. Our daughter, as a preschooler, announced one day, "Mommy, it's easy to make *Lieberplatz* . . . all you need is dough, plums, and crumbs!"

Now that we don't eat a lot of white buns, I have taken part of the dough to make cinnamon buns. We have been pleasantly surprised by how well they turn out using the bun dough recipe.

This is one of our favorite recipes for Sunday morning breakfast.

Anneliese says

Health Buns

Yields 5 dozen

- 1 cup / 250 ml milk, scalded
- 3 tablespoons / 45 ml instant yeast
- 3 cups / 750 ml warm water
- 1 teaspoon / 5 ml sugar
- 4 cups / 900 ml freshly ground whole wheat flour
- 4 cups / 900 ml white flour
- 3 eggs
- ½ cup / 125 ml oil
- ⅓ cup / 75 ml molasses
- 1 tablespoon / 15 ml salt
- 1 cup / 250 ml freshly ground 7–whole grain flour
- ½ cup / 125 ml flaxseed

Kitchen Machine Mixing Procedure

1. Scald milk and set aside to cool to lukewarm.
2. Mix yeast, water, and sugar in the machine's mixing bowl using the dough-hook attachment.
3. Mix together whole wheat and white flours in separate bowl. Add half the flour mixture to the machine's mixing bowl and mix on low setting for 5 minutes.
4. Add eggs, milk, oil, molasses, salt, and mix quickly.
5. Add the remaining flour along with flax seed and 7–whole grain flour; mix until dough becomes soft and is not sticky.
6. Continue to knead for about 10 minutes.
7. Cover with plastic wrap and a towel and let rise until doubled in bulk.
8. Form into buns and place on greased pans. Let rise again for about 45 minutes.
9. Bake in preheated oven at 375° F / 190° C for 20 minutes.
10. Remove from pans and cool on racks.

TIP: Serve these buns with your favorite jam and cheese, or even old-fashioned peanut butter and honey.

—Marg

I do not knead bread dough. My first time was a disaster. I literally threw the dough at my husband and said, "Catch" as he walked in the door. He saw the frustration on my face. It didn't take long before he knew how to get his wife to bake bread. He bought me a beautiful kitchen machine, and an electric wheat mill to grind my own wheat. Once you have tasted freshly ground wheat, you won't want to go back to store bought flour. These buns are now a staple in our home.

Marg says

Who's Cooking

Anneliese's Story

In contrast to the stories I heard from my grandmother, my childhood days were peaceful, filled with not a care in the world and lots of outdoor play. We lived in a dairy farming community in southern Brazil, mostly among Mennonites, where my dad was a bookkeeper for the local co-op.

One of my favorite family activities was bike riding. On Sunday afternoons we would hop on our bikes and visit another family to share a cold supper, which was known as *Vesper* in High German or *Faspa* in Low German. For us kids, it was always exciting to find out which family we would be visiting. We didn't know if our parents had prearranged the visits or not; after all, didn't every home have fresh *Zwieback* waiting for unexpected guests?

When we moved to Canada, my parents found similar Mennonite connections. I grew to love even more the relaxed, holiday feel of Sundays. During the week Dad studied by night and worked by day and mom cleaned houses. It was understandable that she was tired by the weekend. She taught me that work comes before play. While I cleaned the house, she would be in the kitchen cooking up a big pot of soup and baking food for the coming week.

My parents quickly made friends and continued to show hospitality to strangers. We often had guests after church on Sunday, eating a bowl of soup at lunch or buns and cold cuts for *Faspa*. Our lives were enriched by the people my parents entertained.

Some of this tradition of *Faspa* continued after I married. Setting out ingredients for simple sandwiches on a bun, veggies, fruit, and dessert was the kind of meal that the kids enjoyed. It was easy to have the food on hand to serve company, plus it gave me a break from thinking about what to make.

It's interesting how family traditions develop around food. Today, we still serve *Faspa* to anyone who stops by on Sunday. Our son and daughter-in-law know that they can call at five in the afternoon and sit around our table or kitchen island within the hour. Our girls live out of the country with their families now, but it is a meal they still ask for when they come home.

I wonder, is it really the runny strawberry jam and Havarti cheese, the fresh veggies, the weekly allowance of chips, the pie or the *Platz* that's thought of so fondly, or is it the memories associated with a meal shared because no one has to rush off to a meeting, to a game, or to do homework? For me, it all comes down to the fact that *Faspa* is a meal shared in complete appreciation of just being together, with no fuss and no special expectations.

Cinnamon Buns and Variations

- 10–12 cups / 2000–2500 ml all purpose flour
- 4 tablespoons / 60 ml instant yeast
- 4 eggs
- 3 cups / 750 ml milk
- 1 cup / 250 ml water
- 1¼ cup / 310 ml oil
- 1 cup / 250 ml white sugar
- 3 teaspoons / 15 ml salt

1. In a large bowl stir yeast with 8 cups / 2 L flour.
2. Combine eggs, milk, water, 1 cup of oil, sugar, and salt in a bowl and beat well.
3. Heat this second mixture in microwave for 3–4 minutes until very hot, or heat on stovetop, stirring constantly. Pour over flour and yeast, stirring with a wooden spoon until all the flour is incorporated.
4. Continue adding remaining flour, ½ cup / 125 ml at a time. When the dough becomes too difficult to stir, begin to knead it. At this point, slowly work the remaining ¼ cup / 60 ml oil into the dough. You may not need all the flour. Continue kneading for about 10 minutes, until you have a very smooth and soft, but not sticky, dough.
5. Rub a little oil on your hands; form the dough into a ball, rubbing it with the oil. Cover the bowl with a clean cotton towel and place in a draft free place. Let rise until the dough doubles, about 1 hour. Punch down.
6. Use one of the following options for the dough.

Cinnamon Buns
Yields 4 dozen

- Butter, softened
- White sugar
- Cinnamon

1. Divide dough into 4 equal parts and roll each part into a rectangle.
2. Spread generously with butter at room temperature.
3. Sprinkle generously with white sugar and cinnamon.
4. Roll rectangles up tightly and cut into 1½-inch / 4-cm slices.
5. Place rolls onto greased baking pans. Place close but not touching so they have room to rise.
6. Cover pans with towels and let rise again, until rolls have risen and are touching, about 45 minutes.
7. Bake at 350° F / 175° C for 20–25 minutes or until nicely browned. Add cream and brown sugar topping (recipe follows).

Cream and Brown Sugar Topping
- 1½ cup / 375 ml brown sugar
- 3–4 tablespoons / 45–60 ml cream
- 1 teaspoon / 5 ml vanilla

Stir brown sugar, cream, and vanilla together until you have a pourable sauce. When the buns are in the last minutes of baking, drizzle sauce over them and bake another 3–4 minutes. Watch closely, removing the buns when the topping begins to bubble.

8. Invert onto a rack to cool.

Cinnamon Bread

Yields 6 loaves, or 2 loaves and 2½ dozen cinnamon buns or orange crescents

- **Butter, softened**
- **3 tablespoons / 45 ml cinnamon**
- **½ cup / 125 ml white or brown sugar**

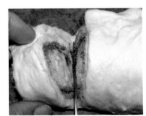

1. Roll a piece of the dough as wide as your loaf pan and about 14-inches / 35-cm long.
2. Lightly spread rectangle with softened butter; sprinkle with sugar and cinnamon.
3. Roll up tightly and place seam-side down in a greased loaf pan.
4. Cover with towel and let rise until double.
5. Bake in 350° F / 175° C oven for 25–30 minutes.
6. Let rest in pan for 10 minutes and then invert to a cooling rack.

TIP: This bread makes great French toast.

Who doesn't love the smell and taste of fresh warm cinnamon buns? I have been using this recipe for over 30 years. When our family comes for a holiday they ask me to bake fresh cinnamon buns, and I am happy to do that for them. During the Christmas season I shape braids and wreaths with the dough and decorate them with icing and candied cherries.

Kathy says

Orange Sour Cream Crescents

Yields 2½ dozen crescents and 2½ dozen cinnamon buns

- Butter, softened
- ¾ cup / 175 ml coconut, unsweetened or semi-sweet
- ¾ cup / 175 ml white sugar
- 2 tablespoons / 30 ml orange zest

1. Roll out 3 pieces of dough into 10-inch / 25-cm circles, each ½-inch / 2-cm thick.
2. Spread each circle lightly with softened butter.
3. Combine coconut, sugar, and orange zest and divide among the circles.
4. Cut each circle into 10–12 equal wedges. Starting with the wide end, roll up wedges to make crescents. Place on greased baking pans. Cover and let rise about 45 minutes.
5. Bake at 350° F / 175° C for 15–20 minutes.
6. Remove from oven. Pour sour cream topping (recipe follows) over crescents and leave in pans to cool.

Sour Cream Topping

- ½ cup / 125 ml sour cream
- ¾ cup / 175 ml white sugar
- 2 tablespoons / 30 ml frozen orange juice concentrate

1. Stir together and pour over hot crescents.

Cottage Cheese Coffee Cake

Yields 9 pieces

- 1 egg
- 1½ cup / 375 ml cottage cheese
- 2 teaspoons / 10 ml cinnamon

1. Press a 1-inch / 2.5-cm layer of dough into a greased 8 x 8-inch / 20 x 20-cm pan.
2. Mix egg and cottage cheese and spread over the dough.
3. Sprinkle with cinnamon.
4. Cover with crumble topping.

Crumble topping

- 1 cup / 250 ml flour
- ½ cup / 125 ml sugar
- ½ cup / 125 ml cold butter
- Icing sugar

1. Stir flour and sugar together and, using a pastry blender, work in the butter to make crumbs.
2. Sprinkle crumbs over the cottage cheese and cinnamon. Cover loosely and let rise for 30 minutes.
3. Bake at 350° F / 175° C for 30 minutes.
4. Remove from oven. While hot, sprinkle generously with sugar.

—Kathy

Cinnamon Buns

Yields 2 dozen

- 1⅓ cup / 325 ml warm milk
- 2 teaspoons / 20 g sugar
- 2 teaspoons / 10 g unflavored gelatin
- 3 tablespoons / 40 g active dry yeast
- ¼ cup / 55 g butter, softened
- ½ cup / 100 g sugar
- 2 eggs
- 2 teaspoons / 8 ml vanilla

- 1 cup / 150 g potato starch
- ¾ cup / 105 g cornstarch
- ½ cup / 66 g white bean flour
- 1 cup / 132 g white corn flour
- ¾ teaspoon / 6 g salt
- 1½ teaspoon / 10 g xanthan gum
- Sweet rice flour

Filling
- Butter, softened
- 1½ cup / 300 g brown sugar

- 2 teaspoon / 5 g cinnamon
- ⅔ cup / 100 g nuts (optional)

1. Mix together in a cup the 2 teaspoons / 20 g sugar and the 2 teaspoons / 20 g gelatin; add the warm milk and stir; then add the yeast, stirring again. Let proof until doubled.
2. Meanwhile, beat the softened butter. Add the ½ cup / 100 g sugar, beating until fluffy. Add the eggs, one at a time, beating after each addition. Add vanilla.
3. Mix in proofed yeast.
4. Mix together and add the dry ingredients all at once: starches, flours, salt, and xanthan gum. Beat on high for 2–3 minutes.
5. Tape plastic wrap to a hard surface. Sprinkle the surface with sweet rice flour. Turn dough onto this surface and knead lightly, using only enough sweet rice flour to make the dough not sticky.
6. Roll out to 24 x 10-inches / 60 x 25-cm. Spread lightly with softened butter.
7. Mix brown sugar, cinnamon, and nuts and spread over the butter, pressing down lightly.
8. Loosen bottom plastic wrap, lifting it to make it easier to roll up the dough. Starting at the long edge, roll the dough as tightly as possible.
9. Pinch the edge to the roll, then cut into 24 slices, about 1-inch / 2.5-cm, laying them carefully in a large baking dish, barely touching each other.
10. Let the dough rise about 40 minutes.
11. Bake at 375° F / 190° C until nicely browned.
12. Remove the pan from the oven, resting undisturbed for about 20 minutes. While still warm, spread with icing if desired.

—Julie

No need to go without cinnamon buns just because you or someone you love has celiac. I have served these buns to non-celiacs and they didn't know the difference.

Julie says

Gooey Walnut Rolls

Yields 12 rolls

Dough

- 1 tablespoon / 15 ml active dry yeast
- 1 teaspoon / 5 ml sugar
- ½ cup / 125 ml warm water
- ¾ cup / 175 ml milk
- ¼ cup / 60 ml butter
- 3 eggs yolks
- ¼ cup / 60 ml sugar
- 1 teaspoon / 5 ml salt
- 3 cups / 750 ml all-purpose flour

1. Place the yeast, sugar, and warm water in a large bowl and let rest for 10 minutes.
2. Put the milk in a 1 cup measuring cup. Add butter and microwave on high for 1 minute.
3. Add egg yolks to the yeast mixture and stir well.
4. Add a small amount of the warm milk and butter to the yeast mixture, stir well with a wooden spoon, and then add the rest of the milk mixture.
5. Add the sugar, salt, and 1 cup / 250 ml flour. Beat well.
6. Add the rest of the flour, a bit at a time, until it becomes too difficult to stir. Remove the dough from the bowl and put it on a lightly floured surface; knead just until smooth and combined.
7. Place dough in a large, greased bowl, cover with plastic wrap and let rise until double in bulk.
8. While the dough is rising, make the filling, the sticky topping, and prepare the baking pan.

Filling

- ¼ / 60 ml butter
- 1 tablespoon / 15 ml cinnamon
- ½ cup / 125 ml brown sugar

1. Melt the butter; add cinnamon and sugar. Set aside.

Gooey Topping

- 1 cup / 250 ml brown sugar
- ⅓ cup / 75 ml butter
- ¼ cup / 60 ml honey
- 2 tablespoons / 30 ml corn syrup
- 2 teaspoons / 10 ml maple flavoring
- 2 cups / 500 ml chopped walnuts

1. Combine the brown sugar, butter, honey, and corn syrup in a small saucepan. Bring to a simmer; then add the maple flavoring.
2. Spray a 9 x 13-inch / 22 x 33-cm pan with non-stick cooking spray.
3. Spread the hot topping ingredients evenly over the bottom of the pan.
4. Sprinkle with the chopped nuts and set aside.

Assembling the Gooey Walnut Rolls

1. On a lightly floured surface, roll the dough to a large rectangle measuring about 12 x 18-inches / 28 x 43-cm.
2. Spread the filling evenly over the dough leaving a 1-inch / 2.5-cm space at the farthest long side.
3. Roll up the dough jellyroll style and cut into 12 even slices.
4. Place the slices on the gooey topping, cut side down.
5. Cover and let rise for 1 hour at room temperature.
6. Preheat oven to 350° F / 175° C and bake in the bottom ⅓ of the oven for 30 minutes or until golden brown.
7. Remove the pan from the oven. Place a large tray or cookie sheet over the rolls to safely and neatly remove the rolls from the pan.

—Lovella

Gooey walnut rolls are such a good coffee break treat. If you want to serve them fresh in the morning, prepare the pan ahead of time, cover it well, and refrigerate. Bake in the morning as directed.

Or, prepare them early in the week and freeze them unbaked. The night before you want to serve them, take them out of the freezer, place on counter and cover with a tea towel. In the morning, preheat the oven and bake as directed.

Lovella says

Peppernut Spice Buns

Yields 3 dozen

- 1 cup / 250 ml milk
- ½ cup / 125 ml warm water
- ½ cup / 125 ml shortening or butter
- ½ cup / 125 ml corn syrup
- ½ cup / 125 ml brown sugar

- 4 to 5 cups / 1000 to 1250 ml flour
- 2 tablespoons / 30 ml instant yeast
- 1 teaspoon / 5 ml ground pepper
- 1 teaspoon / 5 ml cinnamon
- ½ teaspoon / 2 ml ground anise

1. Scald milk, add water, shortening or butter, syrup, and sugar, stirring until dissolved.
2. Mix half of the flour with yeast and spices and add to the warm milk mixture.
3. Add more flour as needed, then knead until dough becomes soft. Let rise until doubled.
4. Punch down dough, shape into buns, and place them on greased or parchment-lined baking pans. Let rise until doubled.
5. Bake at 400° F / 205° C for 10–12 minutes or until golden.
6. Ice and decorate with sprinkles.

—Betty

These are our family's favorite "Easter buns." They are not quite a hot cross bun and not quite *Paska*. My mother made these, and I am carrying on the tradition.

Betty says

I WILL FOLLOW

Trust in the Lord with all your heart and lean not on your own understanding; in all your ways submit to him, and he will make your paths straight. —PROVERBS 3:5-6 (**NIV**)

Every summer we tackle at least one mountain climb. Generally, I don't lead because we would probably never make it to the top. I need clear direction as well as a promise that the difficult journey will be worth the perseverance, even though I often weakly call "I'm done."

Sometimes my beloved takes my hand, walks ahead of me, and encourages me during the steepest part of the climb, always having my best interests in mind. He leads well, with trail map in hand; I follow closely behind because the path is often narrow and I can't see what is ahead. I know he would never mislead me intentionally because he loves me.

My journey in following Jesus is much the same. Because I know that God loves me, I put my trust in him. I tell him that I want him to lead me and be Lord of my life. I listen to his instructions found in the Bible, and realize over and over that I need a Savior, because I am weak in my resolve and too often mess up when I try to go it alone.

I can't see around the next bend and have no idea what lies ahead in my lifetime, but God knows. I will trust him because ultimately my journey leads to heaven. Every morning, I decide to stay on the path as I whisper, "Lead me Jesus, I will follow."

—*Lovella*

Paska (Easter Bread)

Yields 5 loaves

- **2 tablespoons / 30 ml active dry yeast**
- **1 teaspoon / 5 ml sugar**
- **1 cup / 250 ml warm water**

- **1 medium lemon**
- **1 medium orange**
- **1¼ cup / 310 ml milk**
- **½ cup / 125 ml butter**

- **2 large eggs**
- **¾ cup / 175 ml sugar**
- **1 teaspoon / 5 ml salt**
- **7½–8 cups / 1.7–1.8 L flour**

1. Mix yeast, sugar, and warm water in a large mixing bowl. Let stand for 10 minutes or until the yeast has formed a foamy top.

2. While the yeast is proofing, peel the lemon and the orange with a vegetable peeler. Place peel in a blender jar. Remove and discard the white parts of the lemon and the orange. Chop the lemon and the orange into quarters, discard the seeds, and add the chopped orange and lemon to the blender.

3. Heat milk and butter in a small saucepan over medium heat until the butter has melted. Add the warm milk and butter to the blender.

4. With the blender on high speed, mix the citrus and peel along with the milk and butter mixture for 2 or 3 minutes. It will be frothy and light. Do not try to save time here. It is important that the citrus is pureed with only flecks of citrus showing when finished.

5. Add the eggs, sugar, and salt to the mixture. Blend for another minute or until very smooth.

6. Measure this mixture; it should be close to 4½ cups / 1.1 L. If you have a bit more or less, adjust the amount of flour used.

7. Add the liquid to the yeast mixture. Add the flour, 1 cup / 250 ml at a time. Do not add more than 8 cups of flour. It will be soft but the longer you knead it, the more manageable it becomes. Knead for 8–10 minutes either by hand or by machine with a dough hook until it forms a ball and the sides come clean in the bowl.

8. Transfer dough to a large bowl, cover with plastic wrap and a tea towel. Let rise until doubled, 1–1½ hours. Punch down and let rest at least 10 minutes or up to 1 hour.

9. During this time prepare your baking pans using cooking spray, shortening, or parchment paper. Make round, rectangle, or braided loaves and let rise until doubled in bulk, 1–1½ hours.

10. Preheat oven to 350° F / 175° C. Bake the loaves until golden brown. Check loaves after about 25 minutes. Each sized pan will take a different length of time to bake.

11. Remove from pan and cool on wire racks. Make a thin glaze using icing sugar (also known as powdered sugar or confectioner's sugar) and water and decorate with sprinkles. Serve with *Paska* spread (recipe follows).

Paska Spread

- 1 cup / 250 ml butter
- 4 pasteurized egg whites or the equivalent in pasteurized egg white powder and water
- 2 teaspoons / 10 ml vanilla
- Icing sugar, enough to make a soft spreadable icing

1. Beat all ingredients together until light and smooth. Refrigerate.
2. Spread on each slice of *Paska*. Sprinkle with colored sugar.

TIP: Store loaves in the freezer unless you are eating them the same day.

—Lovella

This recipe was the one that brought Judy, Charlotte, Betty and Marg to my *What Matters Most* blog when they searched online for *Paska*. They made the recipe, left comments, and soon we found we were friends.

I have given this recipe to so many people, long before I started my blog. I pass it on as a gift that has been passed on to me. The recipe originated with my beloved's grandmother, Agatha.

It does not have as many eggs as the traditional *Paska* that my mom made but we love the moist crumb that is soft and tender. I still make the egg white icing recipe that my mom made. I mix up a batch, store it in a sealed container in the refrigerator and spread it on each slice.

Paska is our favorite Easter food tradition. Easter is the most significant day in the life of those that have accepted the forgiveness of Jesus Christ. On Easter Sunday we celebrate our risen Lord.

Lovella says

Paska (Easter Bread) Cheese Spread

Yields 8 cups

- 9 hard boiled eggs
- 1½ pounds / 750 g farmer's, dry cottage, or hoop cheese
- 1 cup / 250 ml whipping cream
- ¾ cup / 175 ml butter, softened
- 1½ cup / 375 ml sugar

1. Press the farmer's cheese through a sieve.
2. Separate the egg yolks from the whites, discard the whites, and press the yolks through the sieve.
3. Cream the sugar and butter together.
4. Beat in the egg yolks and the cheese.
5. Add whipping cream and mix well.
6. Line a strainer or cheese mold, if you have one, with 3 layers of cheesecloth, enough cheesecloth to wrap around the cheese. Place the cheese mixture into the strainer lined with cheesecloth and bring up the ends and tie a knot on top.
7. Place the cheese with the strainer onto a bowl with space beneath for the liquid from the cheese to drain. Place a plate on top of the cheese; then place a good-sized rock or brick on top of the plate to help squeeze excess liquid from the cheese mixture.
8. Refrigerate 24 hours, discarding drained liquid occasionally. You will end up with a creamy spreadable sweet cheese spread.

—Ellen

Who's Cooking

Charlotte's Story

I am first-generation Canadian, born to German parents who were born in Ukraine. They fled from their war-torn country across Europe, living first in Germany, then eventually coming to Canada. My father came in 1948 and my mother in 1956, after spending the previous nine years in Paraguay.

My growing up years were strongly shaped by the experience of my parents and grandparents. There was so much loss of home and family for them. Consequently, we grew up very rooted in our faith and family.

As immigrants, my parents received help from strangers and distant relatives. Now our family has a heart for new immigrants and refugees. We also stay connected to family, right down to our third cousins. My husband knows all too well what it is like to start a new life in a new country. He is a Canadian who was born abroad, immigrating to Canada from Paraguay at the age of 22.

I have been privileged to visit Ukraine, Germany, and Paraguay, and see the homeland of my parents, grandparents, and husband. This experience gave me a fuller understanding of what their earlier life was like.

Hospitality was a big part of my growing-up years. Not only did we have people over whom we knew would have us back, but we also took in strangers in need. As a teenager, I sometimes felt uncomfortable having other people live in our home, but now our family does the very same thing. I appreciate the experience and what it teaches me.

My mother always keeps her freezer full. She is ready to feed anyone who comes by or needs a meal delivered. She

shares homemade soup and buns with people recovering from illness or simply out of kindness. She is a great example to our children and me. My father is always ready to be the extra taxi driver, or the encourager on the side at a grandchild's sporting event.

Growing up in a loving home is a very rich heritage that I don't take for granted. I pray that we have continued that heritage. A loving home still has imperfections, but it always allows for open, honest communication, forgiveness, and the knowledge that you are always welcome and wanted.

The greatest inheritance I received is that of a family with a strong faith. Now we have the opportunity to encourage our children to grow in their own relationship with Jesus. I have truly been blessed.

But as for me and my household, we will serve the Lord.
—JOSHUA 24:15B (*NIV*)

Butterhorns

Makes about 2 dozen

- 1 tablespoon / 15 ml active dry yeast
- 1 teaspoon / 5 ml sugar
- ¼ cup / 60 ml warm water
- 2 cups / 500 ml flour

- 2 tablespoons / 30 ml sugar
- ½ teaspoon / 2 ml salt
- ½ cup / 125 ml butter
- ½ cup / 125 ml milk
- 1 egg yolk

- 2 cups / 500 ml icing sugar (also known as powdered sugar or confectioner's sugar)
- Warm water
- 1½ cup / 350 crushed walnuts
- 1 recipe lemon curd (optional)

1. Combine the yeast, teaspoon of sugar, and warm water in a small bowl; set aside to proof.
2. Measure the flour, second amount of sugar, and the salt in a large bowl.
3. With a pastry blender cut the butter into the flour mixture until small crumbs form.
4. Warm the milk slightly and beat in the egg yolk.
5. Pour the yeast and the milk mixture into the flour mixture; stir to combine.
6. Cover the bowl with plastic wrap to seal and refrigerate at least 2 hours or overnight.
7. Place the dough on a slightly floured surface. Pat down the dough, then sprinkle the top with flour.
8. Roll the dough to form a 6 x 14-inch / 16 x 35-cm rectangle.
9. Cut across the dough to make 6 x ¾-inch / 16 x 2-cm strips.
10. Twist and roll each strip into a pinwheel shape. Place on a greased cookie sheet. Option: Add a teaspoon of lemon curd (recipe follows) to the center of each butterhorn.
11. Let dough rise for 1 hour. Bake in a 375° F / 205° C oven for 10–15 minutes until lightly browned. Cool.
12. Make icing by mixing icing sugar with a little warm water to make a thin icing. Dip frosted, unfilled butterhorns into the crushed walnuts.

TIP: The butterhorns freeze really well with the icing and walnut crumbs on. Freeze them on a cookie sheet and then store in freezer bags.

My mom made these butterhorns most often when her Dorcas Ladies Aid friends from church would meet at our house. She would set out her best teacups on her best tablecloth and clean the house as though it was for Sunday.

We always looked forward to these visits from her friends. We would wait patiently and quietly until they left, after which my mom would treat us to the leftovers.

Lovella says

Lemon Curd

Yields 1 cup

- ½ cup / 125 ml sugar
- 1 tablespoon / 15 ml cornstarch
- Zest of 1 lemon
- 3 egg yolks, beaten
- Juice of 1 lemon and enough water to make 6 tablespoons / 100 ml total
- ¼ cup / 60 ml butter, cubed

1. In a small saucepan, mix sugar and cornstarch.
2. Stir in lemon peel, lemon juice, and water. Cook and stir over medium heat until it has thickened and is bubbly.
3. Slowly pour a small amount of the hot lemon mixture into a bowl with the beaten egg yolks. Whisk together, carefully adding about half of the hot lemon mixture in order to prevent the eggs from separating.
4. Pour the warmed egg yolk mixture into the remaining hot lemon mixture. Cook a few minutes, stirring constantly.
5. Remove from heat; add butter. Stir well until the mixture is smooth and glossy.
6. Place plastic wrap against the surface of the lemon mixture to keep condensation from forming.
7. Let cool before refrigerating.

—Lovella

This lemon curd is wonderful as a side to scones with a dollop of Devonshire cream.

Lovella says

Fleisch Perishky is a well-known meat bun among Mennonites. These buns were often served with soup or in place of a sandwich. My sister Rhoda got this recipe from our mom's cousin. It has become our tradition to bake these for our families at Christmas. In the summer I shape them into hot dog buns for our camping trips. They are best served warm with some whole grain Dijon mustard.

Kathy says

Fleisch Perishky (Meat Buns)

Makes 80

- 2 cups / 500 ml water
- 2 cups / 500 ml milk
- 1 egg, beaten
- 2 teaspoons / 10 ml salt
- 1 cup / 250 ml lard, melted
- 1½ tablespoon / 25 ml instant yeast
- 10 cups / 2500 ml flour

1. Mix together water, milk, egg, and salt. Add melted lard.
2. Heat in microwave or on stove until very hot.
3. In a large mixing bowl, stir yeast into 8 cups / 2000 ml flour.
4. Pour hot liquid mixture over flour and yeast. Stir until it becomes too difficult to mix with a spoon.
5. Knead dough 8–10 minutes, adding up to 2 cups / 500 ml of flour, until it becomes soft but not sticky.
6. Cover dough with a cotton tea towel and let rise in a draft-free place for 1 hour.

Meat Filling

- 3 pounds / 1.5 kg lean ground beef
- 1 - 10 ounce / 284 ml can cream of mushroom soup
- 1 cup / 250 ml dry bread crumbs
- 1 - 4 ounce / 113 g package dry onion soup mix

1. Fry ground beef until it is barely cooked. Drain excess fat.
2. Add remaining ingredients; combine well and simmer for 5 minutes.
3. Completely cool meat mixture before filling the dough.

Filling the dough

1. When the dough has risen, punch it down.
2. Pinch off golf-ball sized pieces of dough and flatten in the palm of your hand.
3. Place a teaspoon of cooled meat mixture in the center of the dough.
4. Make a little package by pinching the dough together.
5. Place the filled buns seam-side down on parchment-lined baking sheets.
6. Let buns rise 30 minutes.
7. Bake in 400° F / 205 C oven for 15–18 minutes.
8. Remove from pan to cooling rack immediately. Store in refrigerator or freezer.

TIP: The meat can be made ahead and frozen. Thaw in fridge until ready to use.

Because they are filled with meat, *Fleisch Perishky* must be refrigerated or frozen. To reheat, place thawed buns in a roasting pan, cover, and heat in 350° F / 175° C oven for 20 minutes. They will taste like you just baked them.

—*Kathy*

Bulki (White Bread)

Yields 4 medium loaves

- 4 cups / 1 L warm water
- ½ cup / 125 ml instant mashed potato flakes
- ⅓ cup / 75 ml sugar
- 1½ tablespoon / 20 ml salt
- ¼ cup / 60 ml oil
- 2 tablespoons / 30 ml instant yeast*
- 9–10 cups / 2–2 1/2 L flour

TIP: Instant yeast is formulated specifically for bread mixers and machines, but can be substituted in any bread recipe. The yeast does not need to be dissolved in water. Mix it together with the flour and add to the liquids.

1. Combine water, potato flakes, sugar, salt and oil in mixing bowl.
2. Mix yeast with half the flour; add to liquids and beat well.
3. Add enough flour to make dough easy to handle. Knead very well, until the dough is smooth and elastic.
4. Cover and let rise until double in size.
5. Divide into 4 equal parts. Shape into loaves and place in greased bread pans. Cover with a tea towel. Let rise until doubled in size.
6. Bake at 350° F / 175° C for about 35 minutes.
7. Remove from pans to wire racks for cooling.

TIP: Flour measurements are only a guideline when mixing yeast dough and will vary with each batch.

—Judy

White bread was the bread of my ancestors, and it was the bread I ate while growing up. My mom baked all our bread, several times each week, with no help from bread machines or mixers. In the early years there was only a wood stove, which made it difficult to maintain the right temperature for baking.

The loaves of my memory were not one bit dainty! They overflowed the bread pans, but we enjoyed the huge slices of airy bread with a crispy crust. Though there is nothing like coming home to the aroma of freshly baked bread, I was at times envious of my classmates with their sandwiches made from soft, white slices of store-bought bread, a luxury we rarely had in our home. It turns out I wasn't missing much!

The best treat on bread-baking day was the "fried bread," which we would enjoy at suppertime. Long strips of dough were dropped into hot fat and then dipped in sugar. There was nothing healthy about it but we enjoyed this treat.

Many decades have passed and though I often bake bread, it is rarely white bread these days. Now we know that the health benefits of white bread are not the greatest, and the coarse "peasant bread" with all the whole grains is a much healthier choice. Every once in a while I like to bake the bread of my childhood. My dad still prefers white bread, and so I try to keep some on hand for his visits. White bread is more than a distant memory at my home.

Judy says

Sunflower Flaxseed Bread

Yields 3 loaves

- 2 cups / 500 ml buttermilk
- 1 cup / 250 ml lukewarm water
- ¼ cup / 60 ml vegetable oil
- 1 tablespoon / 15 ml salt
- ⅓ cup / 75 ml honey
- 4 cups / 1000 ml all-purpose flour
- 2 cups / 500 ml whole wheat flour
- 2 tablespoons / 30 ml instant yeast
- 1 cup / 250 ml ground flaxseed
- 1 cup / 250 ml oat bran
- 1 cup / 250 ml sunflower seeds
- 1 teaspoon / 5 ml water
- 1 egg

1. Heat buttermilk in microwave oven until lukewarm, approximately 90 seconds on high.
2. Combine all liquids in a large bowl. Add salt and honey.
3. Combine 2 cups / 500 ml of the white flour with the whole wheat flour, yeast, flaxseed, oat bran, and sunflower seeds. Add to liquids and mix well.
4. Add remaining flour and knead well.
5. Cover and let rise in warm place for 30 minutes.
6. Divide dough into thirds. Shape each piece into a ball or oval. Place loaves on lightly greased baking sheets and flatten slightly.
7. Cover and let rise in a warm spot until doubled in bulk, about 1 hour.
8. Beat together egg and water. Brush top of each loaf with the egg mixture.
9. Using a very sharp knife, score each loaf diagonally 3 times.
10. Bake at 375° F / 190° C for 30 minutes.

—Judy

Brown Bread

Yields 4 loaves

- 3 tablespoons / 45 ml instant yeast
- 7 cups / 1.5 L freshly ground whole wheat
- 5 cups / 1.25 L white flour
- 3 teaspoons / 15 ml salt
- 1 cup / 250 ml seven-grain flour mix
- 5 cups / 1.25 L warm water
- ½ cup / 125 ml canola oil
- ½ cup / 125 ml molasses or honey
- 2 eggs

Kitchen Machine Mixing Process

1. In mixing bowl blend half of the flours with instant yeast; add salt.
2. Add 4 cups / 1 L water and mix for 5 minute on lowest setting.
3. Add oil, molasses or honey, eggs, and 1 cup / 250 ml water.
4. Add remaining flour, kneading for several minutes. If the dough is too sticky, add more flour until the dough pulls away from the mixing bowl.
5. Continue to mix at a higher setting for about 10 minutes.
6. Prepare 4 bread pans. Divide the dough and form it to the size of your pans. Cover with a clean tea towel and let rise 30 minutes.
7. Bake at 375° F / 190° C for about 40 minutes.
8. Remove loaves from pans to cool on wire racks.

—Marg

My Mom always made fresh white and brown bread. This is her recipe, which we have enjoyed for years. I have added 1 cup / 250 ml seven-grain wheat for a crunchy texture. It's a very basic, simple, and yet nutritious recipe. I like that it only needs to rise once. It takes under 2 hours to make this bread from start to finish.

My mom had to work in the field and in the barn. I admire her for her efforts to have available fresh bread and jam for a quick snack at any given time. Early in the morning, you could always find her in the kitchen beginning her meal preparations for the day. She loved to bake and cook for her family.

Marg says

Potato Seed Bread

Yields 1 loaf

- ½ cup / 125 ml warm water
- 1 teaspoon / 10 g sugar
- 1 teaspoon / 5 g unflavored gelatin
- 1½ tablespoon / 20 ml active dry yeast
- ¼ teaspoon / 2 g salt
- 1 teaspoon / 6 g xanthan gum
- ¼ cup / 33 g white bean flour
- ¼ cup / 33 g white corn flour
- ½ cup / 75 g potato starch
- 1½ tablespoon / 15 g millet flour
- 1 rounded tablespoon / 8 g ground flaxseed
- 1 rounded tablespoon / 8 g ground, raw unsalted sunflower seeds
- ½ cup / 125 ml warm milk
- 1 egg
- 1 teaspoon oil / 5 ml

1. Mix the sugar and gelatin in a cup; add ½ cup / 125 ml warm water and stir. Stir in the yeast. Set cup in warm water. Let proof until doubled in size.
2. Meanwhile, measure and blend thoroughly the dry ingredients and set aside.
3. Put warm milk, egg, and oil in bowl of mixer.
4. Add proofed yeast and mix lightly.
5. Add the dry ingredients all at once and mix lightly until blended, then beat on highest speed for 5 minutes until batter is light and very fluffy.
6. Scrape into a greased mid-size loaf pan. The loaf pan will be about half full. Smooth the top with a moist hand.
7. Cover with plastic wrap, and set on top of stove under the range light. Watch carefully because it rises quickly.
8. While it is rising, preheat oven to 350° F / 175° C. Fill a large skillet with water and bring to a boil.
9. When dough has risen to round the top of the pan, remove the plastic wrap. Place a wire rack over the edge of the skillet to provide a steam bath. Set the bread pan on top of the rack. Cover with a bowl large enough to cover the pan, such as a large metal mixing bowl, which will allow steam to surround the risen loaf. Steam for about 7 minutes. The bread will rise considerably more.
10. After steaming, place loaf immediately in preheated oven and bake for 55 minutes. Do not under bake.
11. Cool bread on a wire rack until you can touch the pan, about 20 minutes. Carefully remove bread from pan. If you disturb it too soon, the bread will fall.

TIP: For more good flavor, try this flour combination: substitute ⅓ cup / 50 g sorghum flour for the corn and millet flour.

  The amount of warmth that the stovetop and range light offers is perfect for the dough to rest in this recipe. It is a very delicate balance of warmth that creates the best rise.

TIP: White bean flour is hard to find but you can grind your own from the small white beans that you find in a grocery store. Commercially bought white bean flour, for some reason, smells and tastes very "beany" more so than your own ground flour. It is the bean flour that imitates the wheat flavor and the ground sunflower seeds aid in the toast quality of this bread.

  Use a flour mill or coffee grinder to make bean flour. Grind/sift/grind until there is no gritty feeling when you rub the flour between your fingers.

  Keep ground bean flour in the fridge.

—Julie

The food I missed the most after going gluten free was bread! The rice bread I was offered was not much different than trying to enjoy cardboard. I determined that there must be a way to make something that resembled real bread, something that had the texture, crumb, smell and taste of wheat bread. I experimented with flours and methods, and this is the closest I have come to wheat bread. It is fluffy and soft and smells delicious when baking. Following the recipe exactly is important.

Julie says

Raisin Bread with Apple Filling

Yields 2 large or 3 medium loaves

- 2 eggs
- ½ cup / 125 ml sugar
- ½ cup / 125 ml butter, melted
- 1 cup / 250 ml warm milk
- 1 teaspoon / 5 ml salt
- 2 tablespoons / 30 ml instant yeast
- 3 cups / 750 ml raisins, rinsed with hot water
- 4 cups / 1 L flour, divided

Filling for 2 large or 3 medium loaves
- 4 tablespoons / 60 ml butter
- 4 Granny Smith or Gala apples, chopped thinly
- 2 tablespoons / 30 ml white sugar
- 1 teaspoon / 5 ml cinnamon

1. Thoroughly beat eggs and sugar.
2. Add melted butter, warm milk, salt, 2 cups / 500 ml flour, and yeast.
3. Stir in raisins and then the rest of the flour. If using a mixer, switch to dough hook attachment.
4. Knead for several minutes. Let rise until double in bulk, about 1½ hours.
5. In the meantime, chop apples for the filling; cook them with the butter, sugar, and cinnamon for a few minutes. Do not overcook; they should still have a bit of crunch. Cool.
6. Divide dough in 2 or 3 parts. Roll out as for cinnamon buns.
7. Spread dough with the filling mixture.
8. Roll the dough, tucking in the ends, and place seam-side down on parchment-lined cookie sheet. Repeat with the remaining dough or form plain loaves and place into greased loaf pans.
9. Cover loosely with a tea towel and plastic wrap. Let rise 30 minutes.
10. To give the loaves a glossy look, brush with a mixture of beaten egg and 2 tablespoons / 30 ml milk just before putting them into the oven.
11. Bake at 325° F / 160° C for 40 minutes, or until top and bottom are brown.
12. Dust with icing sugar when completely cooled.

—Anneliese

Rollkuchen
(Fried Bread)

Yields 48

- 5–6 cups / 1.25–1.5 L flour
- 3 teaspoons / 15 ml baking powder
- 1 teaspoon / 5 ml salt
- 4 eggs
- 1 cup / 250 ml sour cream
- 1 cup / 250 ml milk

1. Combine 5 cups / 1.25 L flour with the baking powder and salt.
2. Beat eggs, sour cream, and milk together and add to dry ingredients.
3. Continue to add flour until a soft dough forms.
4. Chill dough 1–2 hours for easier handling.
5. Divide the dough in half; roll out thin on a floured surface. If you prefer softer *Rollkuchen*, roll the dough thicker.
6. Cut strips of dough about 2 x 4-inches / 5 x 10-cm. Make 2 slits in the center of each strip.
7. Gently stretch the pieces before dropping them into the hot oil.
8. Deep-fry in hot oil over medium heat until golden on one side. Flip and fry until the other side turns brown.

—Judy

If you grew up in the Russian Mennonite tradition, you would know that *Rollkuchen* are a tasty, deep fried pastry, served as a wonderful accompaniment to cold watermelon on a hot summer day! How well I recall childhood picnics with big tubs of fresh *Rollkuchen*. It was impossible to eat only one. At some time over the years, *Rollkuchen* and Rogers Golden Syrup (definitely Canadian) became a great team on my table.

My mother-in-law made the best flaky, crispy *Rollkuchen*, which were always a uniform size. Mine are the thicker, softer variety and end up looking rather free-form in size. Though each recipe seems to differ slightly, I've never met a *Rollkuchen* I didn't like!

Rollkuchen puff up beautifully while cooking. Really, they are mostly air pockets by the time they are ready to eat. A totally healthy choice!

Judy says

Authentic *Schnetki* (Finger Biscuits)

Yields 2½ dozen

- **3 cups / 750 ml flour**
- **2 teaspoons / 10 ml salt**
- **½ cup / 125 ml shortening**

- **½ cup / 125 ml butter**
- **1 egg**

- **Whole milk added to egg to make 1 cup / 250 ml**

1. Mix flour and salt together. Cut in shortening and butter.
2. Place egg into a measuring cup; add milk to measure 1 cup. Add to flour/butter mixture.
3. Mix together; turn onto a floured surface and knead until smooth.
4. Form into a ball and cover with plastic wrap.
5. Chill in refrigerator for a few hours or overnight. This is an important step.
6. Place dough on a lightly floured surface. Roll out very thin; spread with softened butter.
7. Starting at one edge roll dough to the thickness of your middle finger, then cut along edge of roll (see photo). Repeat until remaining dough is used.
8. Cut each long roll into 4 or 5-inch / 10 or 12-cm lengths.
9. Bake at 425° F / 220° C for 15–20 minutes, until light golden brown.

—Julie

The *Schnetki*, when broken open, are very flaky.

Julie says

The word *Schnetki* closely resembles the German word *Schnecke*, which means "snail." It is easy to see how these rolled-up-like-a-snail breadsticks got their name.

Schnetki have been my husband's favorite comfort food ever since he's been a child. If I ask him what I should make, I know his answer will be "*Schnetki* and *Perishky*." *Perishky* are fruit pockets made from same dough.

There is a family story tied to this recipe. *Schnetki* always stirs up emotional memories for my husband, memories of the last time he saw his father when he was only four years old. In September 1941, during World War II, Ukrainian officials ordered all men, aged sixteen and over, to be taken from their Mennonite villages and marched to Siberia. Because these men were of German descent they were considered enemies of the state. My husband's father was one of those men forced to march away under guard that fateful morning. He, along with many others, would never see his family again.

Their tearful wives and mothers prepared what they could to send with their departing loved ones. They hastily packed food and clothing, knowing that harsh treatment and extreme living conditions would be awaiting the men in Siberia.

My husband clearly remembers his mother baking *Schnetki* on the outside hearth for her husband. The image of his father walking out of his life, carrying the *Schnetki*, is indelibly imprinted in my husband's memory.

Julie says

Bread FOR THE *Journey*

More than Bread

Jesus answered, "It is written: 'Man shall not live on bread alone, but on every word that comes from the mouth of God.'" —MATTHEW 4:4B (*NIV*)

My grandmother loved to eat bread in any form! She baked double-decker buns (*Zwieback*) and enough white bread to feed an army. But more than bread, she loved her German Bible, which I now have, complete with all her notations.

I treasure her Bible; it is a constant reminder that life is about so much more than the bread we eat!

We were created to enjoy an ongoing relationship with God. That relationship is not fed by the good foods we eat on a daily basis but by reading God's Word, and hearing what he has to say to us.

Jesus said . . . "For the bread of God is the bread that comes down from heaven and gives life to the world." —JOHN 6:32-33 (*NIV*)

Jesus is the bread we really need!

—*Judy*

Cheese Straws

Yields 4 dozen

- ½ cup / 140 g brown rice flour
- ¼ cup / 30 g tapioca starch
- ¼ cup / 35 g potato starch
- 1 teaspoon / 6 g xanthan gum
- 1 teaspoon / 6 g dry mustard
- ½ teaspoon / 4 g salt
- 1 cup / 80 g grated cheese
- ½ cup / 115 g butter
- 3 tablespoons / 45 ml water
- 1 teaspoon / 5 ml Worcestershire sauce (make sure the Worcestershire sauce is gluten free or make your own)

1. Combine first 7 ingredients in a bowl. Mix and cut in the butter.
2. Add cold water and Worcestershire sauce. Add more water, if necessary until dough is easy to handle.
3. Sprinkle a small amount of sweet rice flour onto a flat surface. Roll dough into a thin sheet. Cut into 5 x ½-inch / 15 x 1.5-cm strips and twist each strip.
4. Put on pan and chill in refrigerator for ½ hour or more.
5. Bake at 450° F / 230° C for 10–15 minutes, or until golden brown.

TIP: These cheese straws are delicious when served alone as a snack, or when eaten with salad or soup.

—Julie

I got this recipe from a coworker many years ago, and I adapted it to make it gluten free. For the original recipe, just substitute all the flours with 1 cup / 250 ml wheat flour and leave out the xanthan gum. With wheat flour the dough is much easier to twist into straws, but do the best you can with the gluten-free dough. It handles quite well.

Julie says

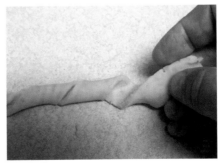

I have taught women's groups at several churches how to make this recipe. It has been deemed a fantastic recipe, and is so much fun to do together in a large group. It's easier to make these twists than it looks, and they are worth the effort. You will be so pleased from the time the aroma of baking cinnamon and maple teases your senses until you enjoy your first bite. This is a good recipe to enjoy in fall and winter. Happy baking!

Charlotte says

Maple Twists

Yields 16 twists

Dough
- ¾ cup / 175 ml milk
- ¼ cup / 60 ml butter or margarine
- 2¾–3 cups / 675–750 ml flour
- 3 tablespoons / 45 ml sugar
- ½ teaspoon / 2 ml salt
- 1 tablespoon / 15 ml instant yeast
- 1 egg
- 1 teaspoon / 5 ml maple extract

Filling
- ½ cup / 125 ml sugar
- ⅓ cup / 75 ml of chopped nuts, optional
- 1 teaspoon / 5 ml cinnamon
- 1 teaspoon / 5 ml maple extract
- ¼ cup / 60 ml melted butter, for brushing between the layers

Glaze
- 1 cup / 250 ml icing sugar
- 2 tablespoons / 30 ml butter, melted
- 1–2 tablespoons / 15–30 ml milk
- ½ teaspoon / 2 ml maple extract

1. Heat milk and butter until very warm and butter begins to melt.
2. In a mixer, blend liquids with 1 cup flour, sugar, yeast, salt, egg, and extract on low speed for 2 minutes.
3. By hand, stir in remaining flour to form a soft dough; knead 5 minutes.
4. Let rise in the oven with the oven light on for 45 minutes or until double in bulk.
5. Meanwhile combine the filling ingredients.
6. Grease a 12-inch / 30-cm pizza pan with butter or margarine.
7. Divide dough into 3 balls. Roll out 1 ball to fit the pizza pan.
8. Brush with melted butter and top with ⅓ of the filling. Repeat layers with remaining balls.
9. Place a round 2-inch / 5-cm glass or cookie cutter in the center of the dough and press down to cut a circle.
10. With a sharp scissors, cut 16 wedges from the outside to the center.
11. Twist each wedge about 3–5 times; press down end to hold in place.
12. Cover and let rise until double in bulk.
13. Bake in a preheated oven at 375° F / 190° C for 18–22 minutes or until golden brown.
14. Cool 5 minutes. Remove from pan onto serving dish.
15. While warm drizzle with the glaze.

—Charlotte

Desserts and Sweets

Hazelnut Roll

Yields 12 pieces

- **6 eggs, separated**
- **¾ cup / 175 ml sugar**
- **½ teaspoon / 2 ml vanilla extract**
- **¼ teaspoon / 1 ml almond extract**
- **1¼ cup / 300 ml ground hazelnuts**
- **1 teaspoon / 5 ml baking powder**

- **¼ teaspoon / 1 ml salt**
- **1½ cup / 375 ml whipping cream, whipped**
- **¼ cup / 50 ml sifted icing sugar**
- **Purchased chocolate hazelnut spread**

1. Grease a 10 x 15-inch / 25 x 33-cm cookie sheet. Line with parchment paper and grease again.
2. Preheat oven to 350° F / 175° C.
3. Using a mixer, beat sugar and egg yolks on high speed for 5 minutes.
4. Add extracts. Beat 1 more minute.
5. In separate bowl, combine ground hazelnuts, baking powder, and salt. Mix well with fork.
6. Combine hazelnut mixture with sugar mixture. Beat for 2 more minutes.
7. Beat egg whites until stiff, but not dry. Fold them into cake batter by hand.
8. Spread batter in prepared pan. Bake for 20–25 minutes.
9. Flip cake onto damp cold tea towel, dusted with icing sugar to prevent the cake from sticking. Remove the parchment paper.
10. Roll up; let cool for 15–30 minutes.
11. Unroll and trim off crusty edges if necessary.
12. Spread with a layer of chocolate hazelnut spread. Cover spread with a layer of whipped cream combined with the icing sugar. It should be stiffly whipped cream. If the whipped cream is too soft, it is difficult to roll up.
13. Roll up the cake once more and garnish with additional whipped cream and hazelnuts.
14. Freeze the hazelnut roll on a cookie sheet for several hours until hard; then wrap with plastic wrap and seal in a zip-close plastic bag.

—Marg

This is a tiny glimpse of what you will see in our home on Christmas Eve. This hazelnut roll has been a favorite in our home for many years, ever since a friend who could not eat flour introduced it. She shared this recipe with us many years ago and it was voted a keeper in our home.

It takes some time and patience to make this recipe. When I set out to do this task, I make sure I have a morning free. I usually make two rolls while I am at it, but do not double the recipe. I hope you enjoy this delightful roll. Serve it straight from the freezer.

Marg says

Strawberry Shortcake

Yields 8–10 shortcakes

- **2 cups / 500 ml flour**
- **4 teaspoons / 20 ml baking powder**
- **½ teaspoon / 2 ml salt**
- **¼ cup / 60 ml sugar**
- **½ cup / 125 ml shortening, cold**
- **1 egg**

- **Milk**
- **4 cups / 1 L strawberries**
- **1 pint / 500 ml whipping cream**
- **2 tablespoons / 30 ml icing sugar**
- **1 teaspoon / 5 ml vanilla**

1. Sift flour, baking powder, salt, and sugar together; stir to mix.
2. With a pastry blender cut in cold shortening until pea-sized crumbles form.
3. Break egg into a 1 cup / 250 ml measuring cup; add milk to make ¾ cup / 175 ml liquid.
4. Whisk egg and milk; add to flour and shortening.
5. Mix with a fork until batter comes together and feels very soft.
6. Turn out onto a well-floured surface and knead until the dough is smooth.
7. Pat or roll out to ½-inch / 1.5-cm thickness.
8. Using a biscuit cutter, cut out dough, placing pieces on a parchment-lined baking sheet.
9. Bake in 400° F / 205° C oven for 15 minutes.
10. Remove to cooling rack immediately.
11. Slice strawberries and set aside. If berries need sweetening add sugar to taste.
12. In a small bowl beat cream, icing sugar, and vanilla until thickened.
13. To serve, split and fill shortcakes with sweetened whipped cream and fresh sliced strawberries.

—Kathy

When strawberries are in season it doesn't take much to convince me to stop and pick a pail of sweet juicy berries to serve with fresh shortcake. Fresh raspberries and peaches make perfect choices as the fruit seasons change.

Kathy says

This is a favorite dessert at our house. I first had it in Australia, where it is considered their national dessert. I believe New Zealand also lays claim to *Pavlova* so you could say it is a "down under" favorite. Apparently, this dessert was developed to tempt the famous Russian ballerina Anna Pavlova, hence the name.

Bev says

Pavlova (Meringue Dessert)

Serves 6–8

- 3 (large) egg whites at room temperature
- ⅓ cup / 75 ml sugar (1st amount)
- 1 teaspoon / 5 ml vinegar
- ½ teaspoon / 2 ml vanilla

- ⅔ cup / 150 ml sugar (2nd amount)
- 2 teaspoons / 10 ml cornstarch
- 8 ounce / 250 ml carton whipping cream
- 2 tablespoons / 30 ml icing sugar

- ½ teaspoon / 2 ml vanilla
- Fruit: fresh berries, fresh or canned peaches, nectarines, pineapple, kiwi, plums or a combination of fruit

1. Beat egg whites until stiff peaks begin to form. Add first amount of sugar, a few tablespoons at a time, beating well between additions. Check that the sugar has dissolved before adding the next amount by tasting the meringue. You should not taste any grains of sugar.
2. Beat in vinegar and vanilla.
3. Mix cornstarch with the second amount of sugar, adding it in small amounts, and beating well between each addition until meringue is very thick and most of the sugar is dissolved.
4. Cut a round of parchment paper to fit a pizza pan. Sprinkle the pan with a bit of water before putting the parchment down, so it sticks to the pan. Or use lightly buttered foil.
5. Pile the meringue onto the parchment in a circle about the size of a dinner plate. Using a spatula or spoon, push the meringue to the outside edges and indent the center so it is slightly lower than the sides.
6. Place in center of oven at 300° F / 150° C and bake for 1 hour. Then turn off oven leaving the meringue to cool in the oven overnight or until the oven is completely cold.
7. A few hours ahead or just before serving, whip cream with icing sugar and vanilla until soft peaks form.
8. Pile the whipped cream into the center indentation of the *Pavlova*.
9. To serve, top the *Pavlova* with cut-up fruit, or arrange fruit slices in a circular design. Do not put the fruit on until just before serving or the meringue will soften.
10. Cut into wedges to serve.

—Bev

Blaetter Torte (Napoleon Torte)

Serves 12

Cake dough

- ¼ cup / 60 ml butter, softened
- ½ cup / 125 ml sugar
- 2 large eggs, slightly beaten
- ¾ cup / 175 ml whipping cream
- 1 teaspoon / 5 ml baking powder
- ½ teaspoon / 2 ml baking soda
- Dash salt
- 1 tablespoon / 15 ml cornstarch
- 2¼ cups / 560 ml flour

1. Mix together the sugar and soft butter in a medium mixing bowl.
2. Add eggs and cream; stir until well combined.
3. Add the dry ingredients and stir until the dry ingredients are absorbed.
4. Place the dough onto a slightly floured surface and shape it into a roll. Wrap the dough in plastic wrap and refrigerate for several hours. The dough will be soft but as the butter hardens again, it will become manageable to roll.
5. Turn the dough onto a floured surface and divide it into 7 equal parts.
6. Cut 2 pieces of parchment paper to fit onto 2 cookie sheets. Dust 1 piece of parchment with flour. Roll the dough out to form a circle on the paper. Place an 8–9-inch / 20–22-cm round plate over the dough and, with a sharp knife, cut around the plate to make a perfect circle. Transfer the parchment paper onto the cookie sheet and bake in a preheated oven at 400° F / 205° C for 10 minutes or until lightly browned.
7. Remove the torte layer to a cooling rack. Repeat the process with the remaining pieces of dough, alternating the cookie sheets.
8. Bake the leftover pieces of dough that you cut away. When cool, crush them with a rolling pin and use for the topping crumbs.

Custard Ingredients

- 5 tablespoons / 75 ml cornstarch
- ½ cup sugar / 125 ml
- 4½ cups / 1.1 L whole milk
- 3 egg yolks, slightly beaten
- 2 tablespoons / 30 ml butter

1. Heat the milk in a medium saucepan until it begins to simmer.
2. Combine the sugar and cornstarch in a small bowl; gradually add to the milk, whisking to avoid lumps.
3. Add a small amount of the warm milk mixture to the beaten egg yolks and then whisk the egg mixture into the warm milk.
4. Continue to stir over medium heat until the custard just comes to a boil.
5. Remove from heat, add the butter and stir every few minutes while it cools.

My Auntie Lorena Betty made this torte for every family gathering. I looked forward to seeing it on the *Faspa* table. It is comforting to know that an auntie will bring a family favorite to the table. To me, it was just another way she showed her love. Eventually I asked her for the recipe and began to make it myself.

Lovella says

Assembling the Torte

1. While the custard is still warm, divide it evenly between torte layers, spreading to the edge of each torte layer.
2. Allow the custard to cool about 10 minutes. Then carefully place the torte layers one on top of the other, creating a stack.
3. Sprinkle the crumbs over the top layer.
4. Refrigerate in a large plastic container with a lid or wrap it in plastic wrap while the layers soften.
5. Check the torte after the first hour to be sure it is not leaning.

TIP: Make the torte at least 8–10 hours before serving or, preferably, make it a day before serving.

Keep the torte well covered in the refrigerator to avoid it taking on the refrigerator's odors. Because this torte easily absorbs odors be careful that your refrigerator is free of any strong smelling foods. You would not want your torte to taste like smoked bacon or onion!

—Lovella

Boden Torte (Fruit Flan)

Serves 12

- ½ cup / 125 ml sugar
- 3 tablespoons / 45 ml butter
- 1 egg
- 1 cup / 250 ml flour
- 2 teaspoons / 10 ml vanilla or a package of vanilla sugar
- 1 teaspoon / 5 ml baking powder
- ¼ cup / 60 ml milk

1. Beat sugar and butter together until light and creamy.
2. Add egg and vanilla and beat well.
3. Sift together flour and baking powder; fold into the butter mixture.
4. Add milk and stir together until it forms a ball. Dough will be sticky.
5. Grease and flour a *Boden torte* or flan pan.
6. Pat the mixture into the pan, using wet, not greased hands.
7. Bake at 350° F / 175° C for 15–18 minutes or until golden brown.
8. Cool in pan for 5 minutes. Invert onto a plate or cake rack to cool.
9. Fill with your favorite fruit. If you use fresh fruit, glaze with a good commercial brand fruit glaze or melted apple jelly. If you use canned fruit or fruit that has been frozen and has juice, make a glaze using the fruit juices (recipe follows).
10. Serve with whipped cream.

Glaze

- 1 tablespoon / 15 ml cornstarch, dissolved in a little cold water
- ½ cup / 125 ml fruit syrup

1. Boil mixture for 2–3 minutes until the raw taste of the starch is cooked and the mixture is clear, not cloudy.
2. Cool for a few minutes and brush over fruit.

—Charlotte

This recipe is more like a sugar cookie than a light cake. It has a firm texture and does not get soggy with the fruit in it. My mother has been baking this for years. In fact it was the dessert at their wedding over 50 years ago. She baked all the *Boden tortes* herself, and, as a result, didn't bake them for many years after that. However, she has made them many times since then, serving them for Sunday *Faspa* when we were growing up. Now I carry on the tradition.

Boden tortes can be filled with your favorite combination of fresh fruits (as pictured) or canned peaches. My favorite continues to be the peaches.

Charlotte says

LIFT UP YOUR HANDS

I urge, then, first of all, that petitions, prayers, intercession and thanksgiving be made for all people—for kings and all those in authority, that we may live peaceful and quiet lives in all godliness and holiness. This is good, and pleases God our Savior, who wants all people to be saved and to come to a knowledge of the truth. For there is one God and one mediator between God and mankind, the man Christ Jesus, who gave himself as a ransom for all people. This has now been witnessed to at the proper time. And for this purpose I was appointed a herald and an apostle—I am telling the truth, I am not lying—and a true and faithful teacher of the Gentiles. Therefore I want men everywhere to pray, lifting up holy hands without anger or disputing. —1 TIMOTHY 2:1-8 (*NIV*)

I paired this photo with this Bible passage because the tulips look like they are lifting their heads to heaven, and it reminded me of prayer: lifting our heads, eyes, thoughts, and hands to the God who created us and taught us how to pray.

Just as this field of tulips with their flowers raised high are beautiful for us to enjoy, I believe our prayers, intercessions, and thanksgivings are beautiful to our God.

—Ellen

Pastry for Pie or *Platz* (Coffee Cake)

Yields 1 large double-crusted pie, 2 single crusts, or 1 base for the Platz variation

- ½ cup / 55 g tapioca starch
- ½ cup / 60 g cornstarch
- ¼ cup / 35 g potato starch (not potato flour)
- 1 cup / 125 g sweet rice flour
- ½ teaspoon / 4 g salt
- Dash / 1 g sugar
- ½ cup / 115 g butter
- 1 rounded teaspoon / 6 g xanthan gum
- ½ cup / 115 g shortening
- 1 egg
- 1 tablespoon / 15 ml vinegar
- 4 tablespoons / 60 ml ice water
- Sweet rice flour

1. Blend well together the starches, flour, xanthan gum, salt, and sugar.
2. Cut in butter and shortening.
3. Beat egg; add vinegar and ice water.
4. Stir into flour mixture, forming a ball. It may seem a little dry at first but it should, with kneading, work into a smooth ball. With too much water the crust will not brown or become flaky.
5. Refrigerate dough for 1 hour or more to chill.
6. Roll out between wax paper dusted with sweet rice flour. Tape the wax paper to a flat surface to keep from sliding. Peel off top layer of wax paper, flip over onto pie plate and then carefully peel off the other layer of wax paper and fit pastry into pie shell. Flute edges for single crust pie. For double crust pie, add filling and then top with top crust before trimming and fluting edges.
7. Bake at 375° F / 190° C about 45 minutes or until lightly browned.

Fruit *Platz* Variation

Yields 15 pieces

- **4 tablespoons / 30 g instant tapioca**
- **2 tablespoons / 15 g cornstarch**
- **⅓ cup / 65 g sugar**
- **Fruit: apricots, plums, or apples**

1. Roll out the pastry dough using the same method as above to fit a 9 x 12-inch / 23 x 32-cm cake pan, making allowance for the dough to come up on the sides. Use leftover dough to make some tart shells.
2. Sprinkle the bottom of the pan with instant tapioca. Add the cornstarch if the fruit is very juicy. Sprinkle with sugar, unless fruit is very sweet.
3. Cover bottom with fruit. If using apricots or plums, cut in half and place cut side down. If using apples, slice them first.
4. Add crumb topping (recipe follows).
5. Bake at 375° F / 190° C until crumbs are browned.

Crumb Topping

- **1 cup / 200 g white sugar**
- **⅔ cup / 90 g brown rice flour**
- **⅓ cup / 50 g potato starch**
- **½ teaspoon / 3 g baking powder**
- **1 envelope / 9 g vanilla sugar**
- **1 egg, beaten**
- **⅓ cup / 75 g butter, melted**

1. Mix dry ingredients together in bowl.
2. Make a well in the center of dry ingredients and add the beaten egg.
3. Mix quickly until the mixture is crumbly.
4. Sprinkle the mixture over the fruit in baking pan.
5. Drizzle melted butter on top of the crumbs.

—Julie

Obst Kuchen (Coffee Cake)

Yields 20 squares

- 2 cups / 500 ml flour
- 3½ teaspoons / 17 ml baking powder
- 4 tablespoons / 60 ml sugar
- 2 tablespoons / 30 ml butter
- 1 cup / 250 ml whipping cream

- 1 egg, slightly beaten
- 4 cups / 900 ml rhubarb, washed and cut up, or cherries, blueberries, apricots, peaches, or apples

1. Mix together dry ingredients. Mix in butter with a pastry blender.
2. Add cream and slightly beaten egg; stir with a fork until it comes together in a ball.
3. With wet hands, pat out dough onto a greased 10 x 15-inch / 25 x 38-cm pan. The dough may be a little sticky.
4. Cover dough with a layer of rhubarb or any of your favorite seasonal fruit.
5. Top with crumbles.

Crumbles

- 1½ cup / 375 ml sugar
- 1½ cup / 375 ml flour

- ½ cup / 125 ml very soft butter

1. Mix sugar and flour; cut in butter with a pastry blender until crumbly.
2. Sprinkle this mixture over fruit.
3. Bake at 375° F / 190° C for 30 minutes.
4. Cool 10 minutes and drizzle icing over the top. Or skip the icing and serve warm with ice cream.

—Betty

This *Platz* is a favorite recipe that I often make. It makes a good amount to take to a pot-luck meal or any large gathering of family and friends. I remember that, as a young girl picking fresh fruit from the bushes, I would anticipate the *Platz* or pie that my mother would bake. As the delicious aroma wafted out of the oven, we could hardly wait to dig into the *Platz*.

Betty says

Bienenstich (Bee Sting Cake)

Yields 24 good-sized servings or 48 small servings

- 1 cup / 250 ml milk
- 2 tablespoons / 30 ml butter
- 5 eggs
- 1½ cup / 375 ml sugar
- 1 teaspoons / 5 ml vanilla
- 2¼ cups / 560 ml flour
- 1 tablespoon / 15 ml baking powder
- ¼ teaspoon / 1 ml salt

1. Grease 2 9-inch / 22-cm spring-form pans or 2 9-inch / 22-cm square pans or 1 large 11 x 17-inch / 28 x 43-cm cookie sheet. Line with wax paper and grease again.
2. Scald milk, stir in the butter and set aside.
3. In a large mixing bowl beat eggs, gradually adding the sugar. Continue beating until mixture is thick and light in color. Add vanilla.
4. Stir in combined dry ingredients.
5. Slowly add hot liquids, folding in until just mixed; batter should be light.
6. Pour into prepared pan(s).
7. Bake at 350° F / 175° C for 20 minutes, until golden. Spread immediately with topping (recipe follows).

Topping

- 4 tablespoons / 60 ml butter
- ⅝ cup / 155 ml brown sugar
- 6 tablespoons / 90 ml whipping cream
- 1½ cup / 375 ml long shred coconut
- 1½ cup / 375 ml almonds, sliced

1. Melt butter; add remaining ingredients.
2. Spread topping evenly over the cake(s), using a fork and going right to the edges.
3. Return cake(s) to oven. Broil the topping for about 2 minutes, or until golden. Watch the process to make sure the topping bubbles and broils evenly, turning the pans if necessary.
4. Cool completely to let topping harden. For easier slicing, freeze slightly before filling.

Filling

- 2 cups / 500 ml whipping cream
- 1 tablespoon / 15 ml sugar
- 2 tablespoons / 30 ml instant vanilla pudding powder

1. Beat all ingredients together until stiff.

To Assemble

If the cake is baked in spring form pans, simply remove rims or lift cakes out onto a flat surface.

1. With a serrated knife, slice horizontally through each cake.
2. Lift top and spread bottom layer with filling.
3. Return cakes to pans or serving plate and add top layer. It will slice into serving pieces easier once it is slightly frozen.

If the cake is baked on one large sheet, it can be more tricky, but the same procedure can be followed or use this method:

1. Spread a clean tea towel over the top. Holding the towel in place, flip the pan upside down onto a flat surface.
2. Remove wax paper and slice horizontally through the upside-down cake. Cover cake with pan and flip back, holding towel in place. Slide hands under top layer, lift carefully, and place on flat surface.
3. Cover with filling and carefully replace the top.

TIP: This cake freezes very well and slices easily once partially thawed.

—Anneliese

Summer Fruit Pies

Pastry for One Double Crust Pie

- **1⅔ cup / 400 ml flour**
- **¾ teaspoon / 4 ml salt**
- **⅔ cup / 150 ml lard**
- **4 tablespoons / 60 ml cold water**

1. Combine flour, salt, and lard in a medium bowl. With a pastry blender, cut lard into flour until the size of large peas.
2. Sprinkle the mixture with water. Stir with fork, in circular motion, until there are no more loose crumbs. It may seem too dry at first, but just keep stirring.
3. Shape dough into a ball with your hands. Divide in half.
4. Turn out onto a floured surface. Pat and shape with hands into a circular shape, then roll out a little larger than the pie plate, adding a small amount of flour if it sticks.
5. Roll the dough onto the rolling pin and then carefully unroll into pie plate. The bottom crust should be higher than edge of pie plate.

Fruit Filling for Deep Double Crust Pie

1. Brush unbaked bottom crust with slightly beaten egg white to keep it from getting soggy.
2. Fill with 5–6 cups / 1.25–1.5 L fresh or frozen fruit.
3. Mix sugar and flour well; sprinkle over fruit. The amounts will vary depending on tartness of fruit and taste preference (see suggestions for ratios below). Shake or tap the pan so sugar disperses a bit, or, if preferred, mix all filling ingredients before placing in the shell.
4. Cover with second crust. Fold top crust over side of bottom crust. Pinch the two layers together as you flute them.
5. Brush top crust with beaten egg white and cut small slits into the crust.
6. Bake at 400° F / 205° C for 15 minutes. Reduce heat to 350° F / 175° C and bake for another 60 minutes or until juice bubbles through slits.

Basic Sugar/Flour Ratio and Fruit Suggestions for Five Cups of Fruit

- Blueberries: Some lemon rind, ½ cup / 125 ml sugar, and 4 tablespoons / 60 ml flour
- Peaches: ½ cup / 125 ml sugar, 3 tablespoons / 45 ml flour, and 3 tablespoons / 45 ml tapioca. Toss with peeled and sliced peaches before filling shell.
- Blackberries: Lemon zest, ¾ cup / 175 ml sugar, 4 tablespoons / 60 ml flour, and 4 tablespoons / 60 ml tapioca
- Apples: ½ cup / 125 ml brown sugar, 1 teaspoon / 5 ml cinnamon, and 2 tablespoons / 30 ml flour. Toss with 6 peeled and sliced apples before filling shell.

Freezing Unbaked Pies
Yields 4 double crusts for foil plate pies

- **1 pound / 500 g lard (can substitute half with butter), room temperature**
- **5½ cups / 1375 ml flour**
- **2½ teaspoons / 12 ml salt**
- **¾ cup / 175 ml water plus 1 tablespoon / 15 ml vinegar**
- **Fruit filling**
- **Egg white**

1. Mix and shape the dough into a ball. Cut into quarters to make 4 balls. Divide each ball in half again. Roll balls to make 8 crusts.
2. Brush the bottom crusts with an egg wash, made by beating an egg white and spreading it evenly over the dough.
3. Cover the bottom crust with fruit filling. If using foil pie plates, use slightly less fruit and sugar mixture than listed in the ratios because foil plates are smaller than glass ones. Cover fruit with top crust, brushing with egg wash.
4. Freeze unbaked egg washed pies and then store in plastic bags.
5. To bake, place frozen, unbaked pie in preheated 400° F / 205° C oven. Bake 15 minutes, then turn oven to 350° F / 175° C and bake until juices bubble out, about 60 additional minutes.

—Anneliese

Lemon Meringue Pie

Serves 8

- 1 10-inch / 24-cm baked pie shell

Meringue
- 5 large egg whites
- 2 teaspoons / 10 ml cornstarch
- ½ teaspoon / 2 ml cream of tartar
- ½ cup / 125 ml white sugar

Filling
- 1 cup / 250 ml white sugar
- ⅓ cup / 75 ml cornstarch
- 1 tablespoon flour / 15 ml flour
- 1¾ cup / 400 ml water
- 4 egg yolks
- Zest of 1 lemon
- ½ cup / 125 ml fresh lemon juice (about 2 lemons plus water if necessary)
- ¼ teaspoon / 1 ml salt
- ¼ cup / 60 ml butter

Because we get eggs from our own hens, I have lots of opportunity to experiment with meringue pies. A meringue pie will not weep when it cools if you gently pile the meringue onto the filling when it is very hot.

Lovella says

1. Separate the eggs.
2. Put the egg whites into a large clean metal or glass bowl. There can be no trace of yolk or grease in the bowl or they will not successfully whip.
3. Combine the cornstarch and cream of tartar; add to the egg whites.
4. Using a hand mixer, beat the egg white mixture, adding the sugar one teaspoon at a time until stiff peaks form. Set aside.
5. Preheat oven to 325° F / 160° C.
6. Prepare filling. Whisk sugar, cornstarch, and flour in a medium saucepan.
7. Add the water, egg yolks, lemon juice, lemon zest, and salt.
8. Stir over medium heat until it comes to a bubbly boil.
9. Remove from heat and stir in the butter. Pour the hot filling into a cooled pie shell. The filling must be hot to prevent the pie from weeping. (When water seeps between the filling and the meringue, a pie "weeps.")
10. Gently spoon the meringue over the hot filling. Be sure to touch the edges of the shell to seal the pie filling and ensure that the meringue will not shrink.
11. Put the pie on the middle rack of the oven and bake for 30 minutes or until evenly browned.
12. Remove the pie from the oven and let it cool on a rack in a draft-free place. When completely cooled to room temperature, chill in the refrigerator for several hours.
13. Use a wet serrated knife to cut the pie.

—Lovella

Who's Cooking

Lovella's Story

Two of my favorite baking activities are creaming butter and sugar together against a clean glass mixing bowl with a wooden spoon, and leveling ingredients with the blade of a knife as it sweeps across metal measuring spoons.

My four older brothers deserve badges of honor for reconciling with me over my attempts at baking, such as the batches of hard cookies that I regularly produced for box lunches. My mom eventually sympathized with them, pointing out to me that cookies, unlike cakes, would not test done by gently pressing on them to see if they would spring back. Every little girl who says, "I want to help" should have a mother like mine who never once shooed me out of the kitchen to make her supper preparation a bit quicker.

The first cookbook that I selected in a store was *Betty Crocker Good and Easy* cookbook, which my dad agreed to purchase to give to my mom for her birthday. I was certain she would love it. I was not quite five years old then, and yet found the book's cover both beautiful and intriguing. I often pulled that book from mom's shelf, admiring the beautifully presented foods. I was fascinated by the perfect rows of varied types of cookies and dainty sandwiches all beautifully photographed and displayed.

Within a few years my parents needed to increase their grocery budget when my elementary scrawled ingredients showed up on the list. Even though the grocery cart was more full when I shopped with them, I was encouraged to continue my efforts in the kitchen as long as I cleaned up my mess. My parents accepted this as part of their lot in life for having but one daughter.

When I was 19 years old, my beloved became caught in the happy trap of my Mom's fantastic *Kielke*. I received a marriage proposal, and soon the kitchen I loved was my

own. After birthing two strapping healthy lads, I rarely had need to wonder who would eat my wares. Terrence and Stuart grew up, became caught in happy traps of their own, married lovely girls, and then blessed us with the most delightful grands.

I feel blessed beyond my needs, living in a country where healthy food is plentiful to serve those I love. When the kids put in a call that they are coming for brunch, I will run to the henhouse and gather fresh eggs. When the grands pull a high stool up to the counter to "help" I smile for I realize that preparing food is not my main passion in life, but it is a means to building relationships.

I'm happy to share my counter and I pray that I will always remember the key ingredients in the recipe of what matters most.

Fresh Raspberry Pie

Serves 6

- 9- or 10-inch / 22- or 23-cm pie crust, baked and cooled

- 4 cups / 1 L fresh raspberries, approximately

Glaze
- 1 cup / 250 ml sugar
- 1 cup / 250 ml water
- 3 tablespoons / 45 ml cornstarch

- 3 tablespoons / 45 ml powdered raspberry gelatin

1. Pile raspberries gently into baked and cooled pie crust.
2. In 4-cup / 1-L glass measure or small microwave bowl, combine water, sugar, and cornstarch.
3. Microwave at high for 2–5 minutes, stirring several times until clear and thickened.
4. Stir in powdered raspberry gelatin. Cool until lukewarm, about 10 minutes if you set the bowl in ice water.
5. Pour glaze carefully over the berries in the pie shell.
6. Refrigerate several hours. Serve with whipped cream.

—Judy

This glaze works well for any fresh fruit pies. Use the appropriate flavor of gelatin powder. Fresh peach pie is a favorite at our home.

Judy says

Apfel Kuchen (Apple Fritters)

Yields 12 fritters

- 1¼ cup / 300 ml flour
- 2 teaspoons / 20 ml baking powder
- ¼ teaspoon / 1 ml salt
- ⅔ cup / 150 ml milk

- 2 eggs
- 3 apples, pared and diced to measure 2 cups / 500 ml

1. Blend dry ingredients.
2. Beat eggs and add milk. Pour into flour mixture, stirring until smooth.
3. Add apples to batter and blend.
4. Drop batter by the tablespoon into hot oil.
5. Cook until golden on one side. Turn and cook until done.
6. Drain fritters on paper towels. Roll in sugar while warm.

TIP: These fritters are also known as *Obstkuchen* or fruit fritters. As another variation, use sour cherries or plums instead of apples.

—*Judy*

In my childhood home, we would have apple fritters as soon as the first yellow transparent apples of the season were ripe. After all these years, I still maintain this tradition. Yellow transparent apples, wonderful cooking apples, originally came from Russia. They were introduced to North America in the late 1800s. These early summer apples do well in our climate and are usually ready for picking by the end of July.

Judy says

Apple Bars

Serves 24

- 2½ cups / 625 ml all-purpose flour
- 1 teaspoon / 5 ml salt
- 1 cup / 227 g cold butter, cubed
- 2 egg yolks plus enough milk to measure ⅔ cup / 150 ml
- 6 cups / 1.5 L apples, peeled and sliced
- ½ cup / 125 ml sugar
- 1 cup / 250 ml crushed cornflakes
- 3 egg whites
- 1 cup / 250 ml icing sugar
- 2–3 tablespoons / 30–40 ml warm water
- 1 teaspoon / 5 ml vanilla extract

1. In a large mixing bowl, combine the flour and salt.
2. Use a pastry blender to cut in butter until it has the consistency of oatmeal.
3. Place egg yolks in a measuring cup; add enough milk to measure ⅔ cup / 150 ml.
4. Stir the egg yolk and milk mixture into the flour and butter.
5. Turn the dough onto a floured surface and knead a few times to blend the ingredients. Shape into a rectangle; wrap in plastic wrap and refrigerate until chilled.
6. Prepare apples and stir in sugar. Set aside.
7. Place the cooled dough on a floured surface. Divide it in half.

8. Roll the first half of dough very thinly to fit over the sides of a 10 x 15-inch / 25 x 38-cm pan. For ease of handling, roll the dough onto the rolling pin and then unroll it onto the pan.
9. Sprinkle the cornflakes evenly over the dough in the pan. Spread with the apple mixture.
10. Prepare the second piece of dough in the same manner, placing it over the apples. Use a small amount of water to patch the dough if necessary.
11. Trim excess dough from sides of the pan. Roll edges of dough together and pinch the dough against the sides of the pan with the tines of a fork to seal it.
12. Prick the top dough with the fork to allow the steam to escape.
13. Beat the egg whites until soft peaks form.
14. Quickly spread the beaten eggs whites over the dough using your hands.
15. Bake in a preheated 375° F / 190° C oven for 35–40 minutes or until golden brown.
16. Combine icing sugar, water, and vanilla; drizzle it over the baked apple bars as soon as it comes out of the oven. Cut into squares.

TIP: The amount of apples is flexible. If you would like your bar with more filling, use more apples and adjust the sugar accordingly.

Rhubarb Bar Variation

In the spring I make a rhubarb variation. Use the same recipe, but replace the apples, sugar, and cornflakes with 6 cups / 1.5 L diced rhubarb, 1½ cups / 350 ml white sugar, and ⅓ cup / 75 ml minute tapioca.

—Lovella

Perishky (Pies-in-a-Pocket)

Yields 24–32

- ½ cup / 125 ml shortening
- ½ cup / 125 ml butter
- 3 cups / 750 ml flour
- 1 teaspoon / 5 ml salt

- 1 teaspoon / 5 ml baking powder
- 1 egg, beaten
- 1 cup / 250 ml milk

Filling

- 4–5 cups / 1000 ml blueberries, or finely chopped fruit such as apples and/or rhubarb

- 2 cups / 500 ml sugar mixed with ¼ cup / 60 ml flour and ¼ cup / 60 ml cornstarch if using apples or
- 2 cups / 500 ml sugar mixed with ¾ cup / 175 ml thickening mix (cornstarch and flour) if using berries

1. Cut shortening and butter into dry ingredients with pastry blender.
2. Add combined beaten egg and milk. Stir with fork until everything is moist. If dough is too moist, sprinkle with a handful of flour and knead gently until dough holds together.
3. Refrigerate overnight or a few hours.
4. Divide dough in half and roll out each half to a square approximately 16 x 16-inches / 35 x 35-cm in size. Cut into 12–16 squares or make 4 long strips.

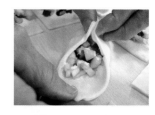

5. Sprinkle about 1 teaspoon / 5 ml of the sugar mixture in the center of each square or about 4 teaspoons / 20 ml along long strips. Top with fruit and another 1–2 teaspoons / 5–10 ml of sugar mixture per square, or 4–8 teaspoons / 20–40 ml per strip.
6. Brush edges of pastry with water. Fold corners of squares and pinch edges. For long strips pinch ends and then along the top.
7. Place on parchment-lined cookie sheets, not too closely together. Bake at 400° F / 205° C for 25–30 minutes. Or freeze the unbaked *Perishky* to bake later. Baking frozen *Perishky* will take more time.

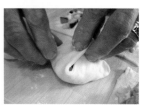

8. If using parchment paper, let cool before transferring to a serving plate; if not using parchment paper, remove before they begin to cool and the juices harden.
9. Do not store in a sealed container except to freeze, because they will get soft. Uncover when thawing.

—Anneliese

Our extended family is blessed to have someone who regularly supplies us with these tasty little "pies-in-a-pocket." I consider it another one of those "labor of love" recipes. I have pretended that I cannot make them, but I'm beginning to think that one day I may change my mind, because they will remind me of one of the most beautiful women in my life, my mom.

Anneliese says

Portzelky (Fritters)

Yields 6 dozen

- **2 tablespoons / 30 ml yeast**
- **2 cups / 500 ml lukewarm milk**
- **1/4 cup / 60 ml butter, melted**
- **1/4 cup / 60 ml sugar**
- **2 teaspoons / 10 ml salt**

- **4 eggs, beaten**
- **5½ cups / 1250 ml flour**
- **3 cups / 750 ml raisins**
- **Icing sugar (powdered sugar) or berry sugar (super-fine sugar)**

1. Prepare yeast as instructed on package.
2. Combine lukewarm milk, butter, sugar, salt, and eggs. Add prepared yeast.
3. Stir in flour gradually. Add raisins.
4. Cover and let rise until doubled in bulk.
5. Drop by heaping tablespoon into deep hot oil. Fry until golden brown, turning once.
6. Remove from oil using tongs. Drain on paper towels.
7. Roll in berry sugar or icing sugar while warm.

Portzelky Variation

Substitute 1 cup / 250 ml chopped apples or chopped dried apricots for 1 cup / 250 ml of the raisins. If you roll them in the berry sugar they freeze well.

—Judy

Whether you call them *Portzelky* or fritters, they are a New Year's tradition for us. It is thought that Dutch Mennonites brought the tradition with them to Prussia in the 1600s and then on to South Russia in the 1800s. To this day we enjoy these tasty little deep-fried tidbits to ring in each New Year. Our Dutch neighbors have the same tradition but call their fritters *Olliebollen*.

Judy says

Who's Cooking

Judy's Story

Some of my earliest memories are of being outside on the farm, alongside my mom, who was going about her daily work. Though she had many chores, I ran barefoot, climbed trees, and made dandelion necklaces. Childhood on a farm is bliss! That all changed as I entered my teens. The bare feet gave way to gum boots. I was expected to do my share of the farm work, along with my four sisters. Driving tractor, milking cows, hauling hay bales or picking corn for market—whatever was happening on the farm, we were part of it. I was not always a willing participant, and looked forward to adulthood and an escape from the seemingly endless duties on the farm.

Before the end of my teen years I married the love of my life. We settled into our new life, still in the country but away from the dairy farm forever, or so I thought! As a sideline, we planted raspberries for the commercial market on our little acreage. Within a few years, we had sixty acres of raspberries. When the raspberry harvest was over at the end of July, we had sweet corn to pick and sell. To ensure that we would have something to do during those winter months we raised hogs on our farm and enough beef for our own needs. I learned 101 ways to prepare corn, raspberries, and pork. We always had a freezer full of farm-fresh produce, including homemade farmer sausage. It was an old-fashioned and good way of eating—from the farm to the table!

When our children entered their teens my parents retired from dairy farming and we were given the opportunity to take over the family dairy farm. At one time I would have run in the opposite direction. Instead, we moved back to my childhood farm, and my children moved into the house I knew so well. They climbed the trees I once climbed, slept in my old bedroom, and even milked the cows in the same dairy where I once milked, a skill I had long since forgotten!

Several decades later, our children are grown and we have grandchildren. Now one of our sons and his family live in the old farmhouse and his children climb the trees and search the furthest corners of the hayloft. They are learning from an early age how food arrives on the table and that there are no days off on a dairy farm. The family farm is almost a thing of the past and I am thankful that our family has been part of that experience.

Though at one time I wished for a life as far away from the farm as possible, one day I realized I was living the life I never wanted—and enjoying it!

> *As the heavens are higher than the earth, so are my ways higher than your ways and my thoughts than your thoughts.* —ISAIAH 55:9 (*NIV*)

Faith, family, friends, food and farming . . . these things are near and dear to me.

Doughnuts

Yields 4 dozen

- 1 cup / 250 ml milk
- 1 cup / 250 ml water
- ½ cup / 125 ml shortening
- 6–7 cups / 1.5–1.75 L flour, approximately
- 1 cup / 250 ml sugar
- 1 teaspoon / 5 ml salt

- 2 eggs, beaten
- 2 tablespoons / 30 ml instant yeast
- 1 cup / 250 ml unseasoned mashed potatoes or prepared instant mashed potatoes
- 4 cups / 1 L cooking oil for deep frying

1. Combine the milk, water, and shortening; heat until shortening melts.
2. Combine 3 cups / 750 ml flour with sugar, salt, and yeast.
3. Mix in the warm milk, water, and shortening.
4. Add beaten eggs, and mashed potatoes.
5. Add remaining flour, one cup at a time, until the dough is soft and slightly sticky.
6. Knead for a few minutes, making sure that the dough remains soft and slightly sticky. If necessary grease your hands to keep the dough from sticking. Let dough rest for 10 minutes.
7. Roll it out to about ½-inch / 1.5-cm thick and cut into doughnuts. Place them on parchment-lined baking sheets and let rise until all the dough is cut out. Fry the doughnuts that were cut out first.
8. Heat oil in a deep saucepan over medium high heat to 375° F / 190° C. To test, use an oil thermometer or drop a piece of bread in. It should turn brown in 30 seconds.
9. Drop doughnuts into oil. Brown one side, then turn over quickly and fry on other side until golden. Do not leave oil unattended.
10. While the doughnuts are still warm, dip them in the following glaze or shake in a bag with icing sugar and cinnamon.

Glaze

- 4 cups / 900 ml icing sugar
- 1 tablespoon / 15 ml cornstarch
- ½ teaspoon / 2 ml vanilla

- Hot water, enough to make a thin glaze

1. Mix ingredients in a saucepan. Keep warm on the lowest setting on the stove.
2. Dip doughnuts in the glaze and lay them on parchment paper to dry.

—Charlotte

Mom's Soft White Cookies

Yields 5 dozen

- **1 cup / 250 ml shortening**
- **1½ cup / 375 ml sugar**
- **2 eggs**
- **1 teaspoon / 5 ml vanilla**
- **4–4½ cups / 1000 ml flour, approximately**
- **4½ teaspoons / 22 ml baking powder**
- **1 teaspoon / 5 ml baking soda**
- **½ teaspoon / 2 ml salt**
- **1 cup / 250 ml buttermilk**

1. Cream shortening and sugar.
2. Add eggs and vanilla and beat well.
3. Mix 1 cup / 250 ml of the flour with baking powder, baking soda, and salt. Stir into the creamed mixture.
4. Add remaining flour as needed, alternately with the buttermilk, until it forms a soft ball. The dough will be slightly sticky.
5. Cover bowl and refrigerate for a couple of hours or overnight.
6. Remove dough from fridge. Roll to desired thickness, approximately ¼-inch / .75-cm. Take care not to use too much flour for rolling or the cookies will be less tender.
7. Cut with desired cookie cutters and place on parchment-lined baking pans.
8. Bake at 375° F / 190° C for 9 minutes and allow to cool.
9. Ice when cool.

Icing

- **3 cups / 750 ml icing sugar**
- **1½ tablespoon / 22 ml soft butter**
- **4½ tablespoons / 67 ml whipping cream**
- **1½ teaspoon / 7 ml hot water**
- **1½ teaspoon / 7 ml vanilla**
- **Food coloring**

1. Cream all ingredients together till smooth.
2. For desired color, add one drop of food coloring at a time, stirring well.
3. Spread icing on cookies and let dry before storing. These cookies freeze well.

—Betty

This is my mother's recipe. I remember coming home from school, greeted by the scent of fresh cookies. I'm sure my mother must have doubled the recipe. I remember the table top covered in cookies, along with whatever space was available in the kitchen. She had a hungry crew to feed!

Betty says

Syrup (Jam-Filled) Cookies

Yields 6–7 dozen

- ¼ cup / 60 ml butter, soft
- 1 cup / 250 ml sugar
- 2 eggs
- ¼ cup / 60 ml oil
- ½ cup / 125 ml Rogers Golden Syrup (or corn syrup)
- 1 cup / 250 ml sour cream

- 1 tablespoon / 15 baking ammonia
- 1 tablespoon / 15 ml hot water
- 4¼ cups / 1000 ml flour
- ½ tablespoon / 8 ml baking powder
- ½ teaspoon / 2 ml baking soda

- ½ teaspoon / 2 ml salt
- 1 teaspoon / 5 ml allspice or mix of star anise and cloves
- Thick jam (recipe follows for thick plum jam)

1. Beat butter, gradually adding sugar, then eggs, individually.
2. Add oil, syrup, and sour cream in order, beating well after each ingredient.
3. Dissolve baking ammonia in hot water; add to mixture.
4. In a separate bowl, mix dry ingredients, then gradually stir into wet ingredients, switching to hook attachment if using mixer.
5. Cover and refrigerate overnight.
6. Slightly grease and flour aluminum cookie sheets.
7. Take ⅓ of the dough from the fridge. Roll out on floured surface to about ¼-inch / .6-cm thick.
8. Cut circles with a 2½-inch / 6-cm round cookie cutter and place about ¾ teaspoon / 3 ml of thick jam (recipe follows for plum jam) on each circle.
9. Fold the circle, pinching together to make a pocket, then turn seam-side down. Place 1-inch / 2.5-cm apart on prepared cookie sheets.
10. Bake at 375° F / 190° C for 20–25 minutes or until golden. Cool and glaze (recipe follows).

TIP: Purchase baking ammonia at some drug and specialty food stores. It usually comes as a lump and needs to be ground to a powder before use. Keep it in a well-sealed container. Do not confuse baking ammonia with regular, household ammonia used as a cleaner, which is poisonous.

Glaze

- 1 cup / 250 ml sugar
- ¼ cup / 60 ml water
- 1 egg white

1. Line cookie sheets with wax paper.
2. Beat egg white until almost stiff.
3. In small pot, between low to medium heat, bring sugar and water to boil, then cook about 2–3 minutes or until it begins to look syrup-like when you drip it off a spoon.
4. Gradually add to beaten egg white, while beating, and continue beating for a few minutes until glossy peaks form when you lift beater.
5. To glaze cookies, begin with the cookie bottom; turn and smooth over the whole cookie. If the glaze begins to feel dry too quickly, wet your hands. Set cookies on wax paper and let dry a few hours or overnight. Store in a sealed container in a cool place, refrigerator, or freezer. These cookies keep well.

TIP: This glaze is a learned art. If it does not work well the first time, try again. It should feel smooth for glazing. If it has a granular texture, it has cooked too long.

Thick Plum Jam for Filling

- 6 cups / 1.5 L cooked, mashed fruit (from about 11 or 12 cut up plums)
- 6 cups / 1.5 L sugar
- 1 tablespoon / 15 ml fruit pectin

1. Wash plums, remove pits, and cut into quarters.
2. Cook plums in a large pot until juices are basically gone.
3. Cool slightly and mash or blend in blender. Measure out 6 cups.
4. Place fruit, sugar, and pectin in a large heavy pot.
5. Bring to full boil, stirring constantly; continue cooking for 15–20 minutes, until it begins to gel.
6. Pour into hot, sterilized jars, and seal. The jars seal automatically if both jars and jam are hot. No water bath needed.

TIP: Because this is thick, it is not likely to drip out during baking.

—Anneliese

Anneliese says

Peppermint Cookies

Yields 10–12 dozen cookies, depending on size

- ½ cup / 125 ml softened butter
- 2½ cups / 625 ml sugar
- 3 eggs
- 2 tablespoons / 30 ml baking ammonia dissolved in 2 tablespoons / 30 ml water
- ½ cup / 125 ml oil
- 2 cups / 500 ml sour cream
- 20 drops peppermint oil (⅓ teaspoon / 1.5 ml)
- 1 tablespoon / 15 ml baking powder
- 1 teaspoon / 5 ml baking soda
- 8 cups / 2 L flour

1. Prepare cookie sheets, preferably light colored aluminum, by coating lightly with shortening and sprinkling lightly with flour. Tilt cookie sheets and tap ends to allow flour to disperse evenly.
2. In large bowl, beat butter and sugar; beat in eggs one at a time.
3. Dissolve baking ammonia in hot water, making sure there are no lumps.
4. Add oil, sour cream, peppermint oil, and baking ammonia/water to egg mixture, beating until well combined.
5. In separate bowl mix dry ingredients; add to wet ingredients, stirring with wooden spoon or using the hook attachment on the mixer.
6. Cover and refrigerate overnight.
7. Divide dough into 4 portions. Roll out to ¼-inch / .6-cm thickness, using a light dusting of flour on the surface as well as on top of the dough.
8. Cut with a small round cookie cutter.
9. Bake at 400° F / 205° C for 10–12 minutes or until golden underneath.
10. Remove onto wire cooling racks. Reuse cooled baking sheet without washing. You may scrape up the flour with a plastic scraper and dust with flour again, but you don't need to keep greasing it for the rest of the batch.
11. If desired, make a thin icing with icing sugar and whipping cream, mixing to a consistency that spreads easily on cookies.

TIP: There are two important ingredients to have on hand for these soft white cookies. The first is baking ammonia, a type of leavening agent, which gives the cookies their light texture. The second is peppermint oil, which does not evaporate while baking the way extract does. Look for these ingredients in a store that carries candy making supplies, a bakery, a health food store, a drugstore, or on the Internet.

Do not confuse baking ammonia with regular, household ammonia used as a cleaner, which is poisonous.

—Anneliese

GOD'S CREATION

The earth is the Lord's, and everything in it, the world, and all who live in it.
—PSALM 24:1 (*NIV*)

During the summer months, Scot and I enjoy camping and hiking. Often we will stop to take in the beauty of God's creation. Whether we are on a mountaintop or walking along the lake shore, nature reflects God's handiwork.

The earth is the Lord's, and he delights in sharing it with us.

—Kathy

Rolled Oat Cookies

Yields 1 dozen sandwich cookies

- 1 cup / 250 ml butter
- 1 cup / 250 ml brown sugar
- 1¾ cup / 425 ml flour
- 3 teaspoons / 15 ml baking powder
- ½ teaspoon / 2 ml salt
- ½ cup / 125 ml milk
- 1 teaspoon / 5 ml vanilla
- 2½ cups / 625 ml quick rolled oats

1. Beat butter and brown sugar together until well creamed.
2. Add flour, baking powder, and salt. Beat until crumbly.
3. Add milk and vanilla; beat well.
4. Add quick oats and mix until well incorporated.
5. Use a spatula to pull dough into a ball in the center of the bowl.
6. Chill dough in fridge for 30 minutes. This firms the dough, making it easier to roll out.
7. Sprinkle flour on surface. Roll chilled dough ¼-inch / .6-cm thick. Using a cookie cutter or glass, cut out cookies, placing on ungreased cookie sheet.
8. Bake at 350° F / 175° C for 10 minutes. Cookies should be lightly browned on the bottom but still soft. Over-baking will cause them to become too crisp.
9. While cookies are baking make the date filling (recipe follows).

Moist date filling sandwiched between two soft oatmeal cookies: I loved it when my mom would tuck these wonderful treats into my school lunches.

Kathy says

Date Filling

- ½ cup / 125 ml dates, chopped fine
- ½ cup / 125 ml brown sugar
- ½ cup / 125 ml boiling water
- ½ teaspoon / 2 ml baking soda
- ½ teaspoon / 2 ml vanilla

1. In a glass bowl, pour boiling water over brown sugar. Add dates.
2. Microwave on high for 1 minute. Stir and microwave another minute, until dates are very soft and pasty.
3. Add baking soda and vanilla. The soda will cause the mixture to foam up. Stir until the foaming stops.
4. While cookies are still warm, spread one cookie with warm date filling; cover with a second cookie to make a sandwich. These cookies freeze well.

—Kathy

Pfeffernuesse (Peppernuts)

- 1 cup / 250 ml butter
- 1 cup / 250 ml brown sugar
- 2 eggs
- 1 cup / 250 ml golden or corn syrup
- ½ cup / 125 buttermilk
- 2 teaspoons / 10 ml baking soda
- ½ teaspoon / 2 ml cloves
- ½ teaspoon / 2 ml cinnamon
- ½ teaspoon / 2 ml ginger
- ½ teaspoon / 2 ml nutmeg
- ¼ teaspoon / 1 ml black pepper
- ½ teaspoon / 2 ml ground anise
- 6 cups / 1.5 L flour, divided

Peppernuts or *Pfeffernuesse*, a traditional Mennonite Christmas cookie, are crispy, spicy, and usually anise flavored. It seems that everyone's grandma had a slightly different version of this tiny nut-sized cookie, which most often has black pepper listed among the ingredients.

The baking of peppernuts is a tradition worth continuing. But let me warn you: they are addictive! The recipe can easily be halved, but no matter how many you bake they will disappear like nuts.

Judy says

1. Cream butter and brown sugar; add eggs and mix well.
2. Add syrup and buttermilk to which the baking soda has been added.
3. Mix together 4½ cups / 1 L flour and all the spices; add to butter mixture. Mix well.
4. Continue adding flour to form a soft, pliable dough.
5. Refrigerate dough. When the dough is chilled, roll it into ½-inch / 1¼-cm thick ropes. Place on parchment-lined cookie sheet. Chill or freeze until ready to bake.
6. With a sharp knife, cut ropes into ⅓-inch / 1-cm slices and place on cookie sheets.
7. Bake at 350° F / 175° C degrees for about 8 minutes.

—Judy

Tee Gebaeck (*Linzer* Cookies)

Yields 4 dozen

- 2¾ cups / 675 ml flour
- 2 teaspoon / 20 ml baking powder
- ¾ cup / 175 ml sugar
- 1 cup / 250 ml cold butter, grated
- 2 eggs
- 1 teaspoon / 5 ml vanilla
- Jam for filling
- Icing sugar for dusting

1. Sift together the flour, baking powder, and sugar.
2. Make a hole in the middle of the flour mixture and slowly add grated butter. Mix well.
3. Add eggs and vanilla.
4. Knead the mixture until the dough is smooth. Divide into 2 portions. Refrigerate for several hours. It's important to have the dough chilled, as it is much easier to work with.
5. On a floured surface roll out the first batch of dough until it is very thin, less than ¼-inch / .6-cm. Use the round base cutter for the first batch. These will be the cookie bottoms. Keep the other batch in the fridge while cutting.
6. Remove the second batch of dough from fridge. Roll out and use your favorite cutters to make the designs for the cookie tops.
7. Bake at 375° F / 190° C for 4–5 minutes.
8. When cookies are baked and cooled, assemble them, using your favorite jam. Spread about 1 teaspoon of jam on the base. Cover with top cookie to create a sandwich effect. Freeze.
9. Just before serving, give the cookies a light dusting of icing sugar.

TIP: Raspberry jam is our favorite filling.

Linzer cookie cutters are available at a delicatessen, and come with a base and several interchangeable cutout designs.

—Marg

Some of you may recognize this German recipe, also referred to as *Linzer* Cookies. These cookies were part of a Christmas exchange years ago, from one of my aunts. My husband was determined to win this gift, diving into the game with a happy smile on his face. He begged me for years to get this recipe. Finally, it's been handed down through the generations in our family. This recipe also takes a bit of time, so guess who I call on to help spread the jam between the layers?

Marg says

Gluten-Free Cooking

Because the success of gluten-free baking depends on consistent and accurate measurements, this book includes the weight / grams conversions for dry ingredients in all gluten-free recipes.

What Is Celiac?

As short a time as five years ago, a puzzled expression was the immediate response of anyone hearing the word *celiac* or *gluten*. Today that is changing as the awareness of this disease is growing. In Canada, for example, it is estimated that 1 in 133 people have celiac disease.

Celiac is an auto-immune medical condition that prevents the small intestine from absorbing nutrients. Gluten's irritation of the small intestinal wall allows food toxins that would otherwise be eliminated as waste to escape into the body and cause severe damage. Cancer or other medical conditions can result.

There is no cure, but the disease can be totally controlled by a life-long avoidance of gluten. Gluten is the protein found in wheat, rye, and barley. It is this protein that triggers the body's immune system to turn on itself.

Searching for Gluten

Simply avoided those gluten-containing flours is not enough. A celiac must read every single label because of "hidden" gluten. For example: the gluten in malt, soy sauce, or packaged foods. Chewing gums can be dusted with gluten, too.

Oats, while they do not contain the offensive gluten protein, are cross-contaminated because oats are grown as alternate crops in wheat fields. There are however gluten-free oats available.

There is a huge list of alternate gluten-free flours that can be substituted for wheat, rye, and barley—and the wonderful advantage is that these flours are full of rich vitamins, protein, and minerals that have been processed out of our wheat flour. The disadvantage is that without the gluten, which is what gives us that wonderful elastic quality in breads, baking with gluten-free flours presents a completely new way of doing things.

Restaurants, while much more celiac-friendly and knowledgeable than they used to be, are still a challenge for those on a gluten-free diet. French fries may or may not be coated with gluten. Some chefs coat plain rice and potatoes with gluten. Sauces and gravies and soups are often thickened with flour.

Gluten-free Entertaining

It is overwhelming sometimes to invite celiacs for dinner, but following a few simple rules makes it quite doable. Serving food that is naturally free of gluten is the easiest way to go—homemade soups, meat dishes, casseroles, vegetables, and fruit are always great. Also, there are many pre-prepared gluten-free foods or mixes available now in grocery or health-food stores.

—Julie

Glossary of Terms

APFEL KUCHEN (OBST KUCHEN): A fruit fritter, usually made with apples in our tradition. It also means "apple cake" in German.

ARME RITTER: French toast

BERRY SUGAR (CASTOR'S SUGAR, BAKER'S SUGAR): Super-fine sugar

BIENENSTICH: A German coffee cake with a baked-on topping of honeyed almonds and a custard filling. Also known as Bee Sting Cake.

BLAETTER TORTE (NAPOLEON TORTE): The Russian Mennonite version of the French torte, which has many layers of pastry filled with a rich custard

BLINTZES: Thin cheese-filled pancakes

BODEN TORTE: Fruit flan

BORSCHT (BORSCH, KOMMSTBORSCHT): In Mennonite cuisine, *Borscht* is a cabbage soup, with beef, potatoes, tomatoes, onions, dill, and seasonings.

BUBBAT (BOBBAT): A batter bread with fruit, often used as a dressing for chicken or fowl. It can also be made with sausage and form a savory one-dish meal.

BULKI (BULKJE): Russian Mennonite white bread

BUTTER SOUP (BOTTASUPP): Similar to potato soup, enhanced with butter and cream

DRY CURD COTTAGE CHEESE: A soft, unripened cheese with white, dry curds made from curdled skim milk. It is often used in the filling for *Wareneki* (*Vereniki*) and *Blintzes*.

EUROPEAN WIENERS: A longer, thinner version of the wiener, available at the deli and usually made from ground pork

FARMER'S CHEESE: A soft, white unripened cheese made from milk, cream, and salt. It is basically dry curd cottage cheese that has been pressed to form a brick. It is often used in fillings for *Blintzes* and *Wareneki*.

FARMER SAUSAGE: A sausage made with ground pork, salt, and pepper and then smoked but not cooked. One ring of farmer sausage is usually about 1½ pounds / 750 g. If farmer sausage is not readily available, substitute with smoked ham or smoked kielbasa.

FLEISCH PERISHKY: Meat buns

GERMAN PANCAKES: Large, thin, crêpe-like pancakes. When filled with cheese and fruit, they are called *Blintzes*.

HOLUPSCHI (HALLAPSE): Cabbage rolls

HOOP CHEESE: A dry cheese similar to farmer's cheese, but made from milk alone

ICING SUGAR (POWDERED SUGAR, CONFECTIONER'S SUGAR): A very fine powdered sugar used to make icing or frosting

KARTOFFELPUFFER: Potato pancakes

KIELKE (KIELKJE): Noodles

KITCHEN MIXERS/MACHINES: Generic term for mixers with dough hooks used when making yeast dough recipes

KOTLETTEN (COTLETTEN): Small, tasty meatballs, usually deep-fried

OBST MOOS (PLUMA MOOS): A cold fruit soup made from dried fruits

PASKA: An Easter bread, made with butter, eggs, and sugar and often frosted with white icing and decorated with colorful sprinkles

PAVLOVA: Meringue dessert named after the famous Russian ballerina Anna Pavlova

PERISHKY (PERISCHKI): Yeast dough or pastry pockets filled with fruit or meat

PFEFFERNUESSE (PEPPERNUTS): A small spicy cookie, often the size of a hazelnut; traditionally served at Christmas

PLATZ (OBST PLATZ, OBST KUCHEN): A fresh fruit dessert with a cake-like base, fruit filling, and crumble topping; usually baked on a large pan

PORTZELKY: A deep-fried fritter, studded with raisins and traditionally served on New Year's Eve

REISTCHE (REESCHE): *Zwieback* are toasted slowly at a low oven temperature until thoroughly dried out. Once cool and hard, they will last for a very long time. They are traditionally served with coffee.

ROGERS GOLDEN SYRUP: Golden syrup is a by-product from the refining of sugar cane and often used as a substitute for golden corn syrup. It is very popular in Canada and Britain, but not readily available in the United States. Use golden corn syrup if not available.

ROLLKUCHEN: A light and crisp fried bread often served with watermelon

RÜHREI: German scrambled eggs that are much like chopped pancakes because they contain flour. They are often eaten with sugar.

SCHMAUNDT FAT: A cream gravy most often served with homemade noodles of any kind

SCHNETKI (SCHNETJE): A very rich finger biscuit

SPAETZLE: Egg noodles or dumplings formed by pressing dough through a colander

SPICE HOLDER: A small metal container available at kitchen shops, useful for adding herbs and spices to the simmering soup pot and easily removed later

SUMMER SAVORY (*PFEFFERKRAUT*): An herb most often used with green bean and pea dishes

TEE GEBAECK: Means dainties served with tea, for example *Linzer* cookies

WARENEKI (VERENIKI): Cottage cheese pockets (can also be filled with fruit); also known as perogies

YEAST: Active dry yeast works best when dissolved in water with a teaspoon of sugar prior to mixing with dry ingredients (100–110° F / 37–43° C). Instant yeast is designed for mixing directly with other dry ingredients before use but also can be used in place of active dry yeast following the active dry yeast method.

ZEST: Tiny filaments of the outer layer of citrus peel

ZWIEBACK (TWEIBACK, TWEEBACK): A soft double-decker yeast bread roll, rich in butter and salt. The two balls of dough are placed one on top of the other before baking, and then easily pulled apart to eat.

Index

Kotletten (*cotletten*), 194

The Authors

LOVELLA SCHELLENBERG enjoys farm life together with her husband, Terry, near the west coast of British Columbia. Having been married thirty-three years, they are in the empty nest stage of life with their two sons grown and married. They are now reaping the benefits with four delightful grands.

Lovella and Terry's passion for seeing marriages thrive has filtered down to their involvement together in a pre-marriage mentoring capacity at Northview Community Church.

She loves to hike the beautiful coastal mountains and on occasion can be found sitting at her sewing machine or in her backyard sipping hot coffee with her beloved.

ANNELIESE FRIESEN and her husband, Herb, have made their home in the beautiful Fraser Valley of British Columbia, where they have raised three children. They are the proud grandparents of seven sweet grandchildren.

Together they have been involved in various ministries related to care and hospitality for thirty years. She is now in what she calls the fall season of her life, enjoying the vibrant colors of the changes this season has brought with it. Her desire is to encourage younger women in their roles as wives and mothers, being grateful to her Lord and Savior for his wonderful provision for such a time as this.

JUDY WIEBE lives with her husband, Elmer, in the Fraser Valley of British Columbia, where she is involved in the family dairy farm operation. She has three grown children, their spouses, and her delightful grandchildren living nearby.

Judy enjoys spending time in the great outdoors, creating things in her kitchen or sewing room, and traveling whenever possible. But her favorite times are those spent with friends and family. She attends Central Community Church in Chilliwack.

BETTY REIMER together with her husband, John, lives in Steinbach, Manitoba. She and her husband owned and operated a farm and garden equipment business for twenty-eight years and are now retired.

Betty attends Evangelical Fellowship Church. She loves spending time with her family and friends and enjoys reading, gardening and traveling.

BEV KLASSEN works with her husband, Harv, in a home-based business in Rosedale, British Columbia. Bev and Harv have three children and five grandchildren; they enjoy hosting family and friends in their home.

When she's not taking pictures, making scrapbooks, or making cards, Bev can be found traveling—either by car or on the back of a motorcycle. Greendale Mennonite Brethren Church has been her church home for forty years.

CHARLOTTE PENNER lives in Winnipeg, Manitoba, with her husband, Tony, and family. They attend Douglas Mennonite Church and as a family are involved in a variety of ways. Charlotte has reached out and served in her community for the past 20 years with the local Crisis Pregnancy Center.

Charlotte loves hosting and being with family and friends. She has a special gift with her hands and uses them to serve others.

ELLEN BAYLES lives in the Seattle area with her husband, Greg. She was born and raised in Los Angeles and completed her education there with a bachelor of arts degree in home economics and a fifth year to earn her elementary teaching credential. She was an elementary school teacher until her first child was born.

Ellen and Greg raised two sons and a daughter. She now enjoys homemaking, traveling, and photography. She and Greg attend Westminster Chapel in Bellevue, Washington.

JULIE KLASSEN'S life was changed because of unexpected health challenges. But every cloud has a silver lining, and Julie is now enjoying early retirement.

Julie lives with her husband, Vic, in Chilliwack, British Columbia, close to their daughter, son-in-love, and two beautiful granddaughters. She enjoys spending time with family and friends as well as reading, writing, baking, sewing, and leading a weekly Bible study group with her husband.

KATHY MCLELLAN grew up on Vancouver Island, British Columbia. She met her husband, Scot, the summer of grade eight at their church youth group. The high school sweethearts married New Year's Eve of Kathy's graduating year. Together they raised their two daughters on a hobby farm in the Fraser Valley. Both girls are married and have added a total of five precious grandchildren to the family.

Together Kathy and Scot enjoy spending time with their family, camping with their grandchildren and friends, hiking, and riding their Harley. They attend Promontory Community Church.

MARG BARTEL was born and raised in the Fraser Valley of British Columbia. She met her husband, John, at a farm sale, and together they continued a farming career. Later in life, when farming no longer demanded her strong support, Marg decided to continue her education and completed her baccalaureate degree, thus giving her new opportunities to work outside the home.

Marg is a sports enthusiast and enjoys traveling. She also enjoys the opportunity to be actively involved in the life of her family, friends, community, and church.

The "Mennonite Girls," from left to right: Marg, Julie, Anneliese, Kathy, Judy, Betty, Bev, Charlotte, Ellen, Lovella.